"CRIME CONTROL & CAPTIVITY"

An autobiography memoir into the character deposition, cultural, & documented events 1999-2020 prior

CORY MORREL

authorHOUSE°

AuthorHouse™
1663 Liberty Drive
Bloomington, IN 47403
www.authorhouse.com
Phone: 833-262-8899

Published by AuthorHouse 02/11/2021

ISBN: 978-1-6655-1671-6 (sc)
ISBN: 978-1-6655-1672-3 (e)

CHAPTER 1

ATROCITY

Tragedy had stricken. Atrocity then burdened. This is where I begin. I have been impacted with much obtuse obstacles I should have excelled through military boot camp training, or, graduated the special forces with honors. I'm a novice author, a freelance writer and a graphic artist with intelligence and high-maintenance distinction of sensible common sense. I discount the genius counter-productive politics and prejudice pride of an arrogant millennial society subduing subnormal the errors self-governing eradication, the antiquated hypocrisy of amicability being renounced. That's why I maintained a good head on my shoulders, the ethics, the morals, polished like a set of brand new shoes just bought out of the shoe store you would purchase on the holidays or tradition of special occasions. This book is my paramount autobiography memoir of the crimes, control, and captivity I underwent that happened to me of the irrefutable duress in much generations. I will digress the background case memoir of the abuse, torment, scorn, cruelty and brutality

1

of the besieged hostile domestic torture I sustained for the record. I have a subtle permanent disfigured injury evident that passed few years, over a decade, that's going to require plastic surgery from another's tangent hysteria. I was in my 30s when this book was written. According to state licensed psychiatrists I was diagnosed Bi-Polar type 1 Mania having mannerisms of schizo-effective symptoms. There were circumstances, perils, and pitfalls I experienced dissatisfied from cognitive disorder of family assault. There were instances where I had been misjudged and misconstrued a physical behavior health condition aspects through cunning ways from individuals' subversion that has had me committed to community control in the corrections system. The result? Subversion. There wasn't any conflict of paraphernalia misuse of adverse content since the day I was born to present day. What I'm guilty of was being a damaged victim from others' malice in unsafe territory. I was in police custody four times from jeopardy and inhumane baker acts misconceived as dangerous. I've always been a pacifist and stayed neutral from calamity. I'm eager to discuss the practical realities of terror I begrudge on a practical level even today. My family that circumvents around me refused to listen to my stories, apparently confused my projected eloquent rhetoric withdrawn. When I speak or elaborate, people that listen to my replies mischaracterized the truth of my opinion, claiming, that I imagine mistranslated facts of what I experience as invalid, unreal, imaged and unintelligent activities as an unpleasant presence of lunacy. But that's not the authentic case. That what I sense, is dysfunctional, but not reasonable by the psychological impact I was contributing by cultural antagonism. What is translated as unusual is misread from family claims. That an ill-judged heterosexual unwell man is falsifying everything he sees, hears, thinks, judges and comprehends evident as a fantasy. I was induced sicker from superior control silenced my Constitutionalism. My comments were ridiculed bizarre, lucid, and impractical testified from my family and surrounding neighbors refused to acknowledge my thoughts with my behavior conscious corresponding my routine code of conduct, as if, I had to be examined permission by opinions and evaluated by an inclusion of appropriate progressive affairs. If you're a Conservative the magnified standards of the case are offended by the progressivism resisting attempts of inept performance to glimpse the opposite observation of themselves. It is the opposite subject that is not examined if subject A that is forced under induced control has natural self-control and subject B doing the stereotyping orders subject A to be analyzed has an element of progressivism emphatically not omitted medical examination. The result is total transformation of character, un-recollection recoil from indoctrination of psychotropic chemical compound agents forced indecision, and demanded institutions. Since 1999 I have been on tight restriction constricting my liberties and national freedoms. I have been under mandated control indoctrination by permanent behavior health checkups regularly of a functioning normal man required treatment of community control through the Sciences of Statism while from my 20s-mid 30s. An acknowledged fact insulting me scrutiny appears to the individual mannerism of any person's mind. As grown man I live home. I lived in Naples, Florida. Naples Florida is a transient state. It's co-dependent on the aggrandizement Capitalism of tourism and senior retirement population. Florida is also a paratrooper military state. 0-tolerance is prohibited and 0-drama is un-permitted with preventive medicine accessible for safety perimeters. People want relaxation, luxury, irrepressible dining experiences and exotic scenery escape beaches. If you want entertainment then New York, Los Angeles CA, Toronto Canada are example foundations for show business. The aftermath of writing 2 books with denied press coverage for documentary or TV appearance, because of my dilemma and mischief legally in the past, I will detail later on in the chapters of this book. The situations held me captive undercut for my career as a performer faded. I couldn't afford a single 1 bedroom in Naples, FL unless I lived with a roommate or shared an apartment. We'd have to split the rent distributed. I would want to work for my own apartment, so I have dating privileges. When I lived in Naples I had to use my discretion in a town of strict restriction, intolerable or impermissible because of the drug, alcohol, and domestic violence history precedence subservient to the cultural decline that descended. There's a density of a court escapade predicament I've familiarized in the system and notated. In 2010 my family and I moved down from my home state of Bergen County, New Jersey to Collier County, Naples Florida. We returned after we left Collier County Naples, FL, 2003. I graduated high school with a specialized diploma and received my GED in 2003 with an overall mastered average of 88.0% 2300 points scored excellent with achievement. Boy, did I wish I took the FCAT, the SATS, and the HSCT to earn a scholarship degree of my choice for a chance to advance forward to an academic college institution selection of my choice, then on to a college entrance exam. The problematic fickle at the time was school guidance teachers with administrators, heavily influenced my mother with drunken hearts and paralyzed minds, persuaded her, I can only attend a vocational school for the handicapped or learning challenged. I proved them wrong. In 2010 I graduated college in Paramus NJ, a Liberal college of academics, excellence, and achievement with an A.A. in Computer Science C.S.T Technology. My degree was excelled in the field of Sciences. It was a Jr. college received my first higher education diploma from our former Dean Principal, that the best of my acclaimed knowledge I remembered undisclosed. I struggled with Math and Algebra. But I was inept intricate more in comprehensive English courses. I registered for mainstream classes frequently each semester that integrated intensity. I was held back 4 years of a 2 year college for failed classes vaguely on the verge of being expelled from the institution. I was obligated orders to take a complicated Biology 101A course or a Geology 101A course, a requirement for credits collective calculated to complete graduation. It was one of the either option decided to pass in order to get my A.A. in Computer Science. I took Geology 2 times. One the first attempted I failed with an F, but on the 2nd attempted I transformed my grade from an F to a B+ almost an transparent A. I passed all 4 semester tests with A's except the final grade with a B average that averages my passing grade to a 90. I had a sprinkling of determination and little push optimism of dynamics. God was on my side to overcome the obstacles. I outsmarted barriers blocking me from comprehensive expectations. After I finished college, I had a part-time job at a fast-food restaurant where I, my mom, and brother at the time lived was a rundown, outdated house in Ridgewood, NJ. We rented from a landlord. We shared a house with 2 narcissistic neighbors, pitiful that the epitomized landlord partially sided favoritism conflict of interest liability against our characters. We moved out. We finally got out of the cold and the corrupt escalating tax-paying North Bergen County stateside of NJ. From the documented events I depicted, the referenced scenario authentic had been an atrocity. The atrocity was just beginning because now that I'm a post-graduated Alumni of a Jr. degree of college. I was entering my adult years. On July 11th, 2010 my brother, mother, and I moved back to Naples, FL. After I graduated high school in 2002 my father died from lung cancer. When I registered for classes at Bergen, administrators validated a G.E.D. wasn't mandatory in the state requirements in NJ to attend a public community college. Department of Education policy was different. Prior in Naples FL, we bought affordable housing. It was a 2 bedroom condo with 2 bathrooms, 1 shower. The condo had only 2 bedrooms instead of 3. I had to share a bunk bed with my brother who had the top bed and I had the bottom bed. I was 26, my brother was about 10, so sensibly to avoid awkwardness fate responded to an episode that developed. I was put out. An indicative incident that also occurred as well subsequent, encouraged me a vicarious message. I needed to be on my own. But the consequences of the awkward trouble didn't appear until we moved 3 months afterwards coming back to FL from NJ, 8 years later September 2nd, 2010. On September 2nd, 2010 after working a part-time job in another restaurant which I lost after 2.5 weeks, I committed a complicit misact of a domestic violence crime. I was arrested and in put jail for 3 days which ashamed I still remember precedent pain in the record. I wasn't right. I felt as if an aspect evil of dehumanizing forces restrained me in fear, as far I only admissibly permitted them to get the best of me. I swallowed my pride and almost 10 years later, I transformed my character in society to stay engineered with transparency following modern day maturity to received enthusiasm, in return of hope, that my past won't haunt my future aspirations by criticism. I had to verbally tell my vulnerable story on paper, testifying my statement to shrink the pain, paralyze the contusion and close the wound on the injury that people will get to know me better to discover what kind of person I am, what kind of character I have, and how I was raised with scruples. I'm not a violent offender. I had to write the vehicle of my injury. If I have something aching me in agony of my soul let the ink do the hollering and release it. If I have an itch, don't scratch it to spread the infection. Just apply the cream. My mom was a victim of a crime that I harmed unconsciously. Partly, I don't even remember, other-times I do. I get disheartened. I took the blame. I was half-guilty and half-innocent, so I pleaded no contest at the trial. I was found partly guilty and did 1 year probation with a 10 week course of Anger Management and 5 months of community service paying back all my fines. Before that time I was also on a psychotropic medication that reduced the condition of my diagnosis feeling poisoned. I was on a derivative that closed my respiratory system compromised to breath. I resisted, because I could not breath naturally. My mom recommended I either take my medication or be kicked out of the condo, to be evicted by police escort. I have had minuscule Constitutional rights by civil liberties being a home dweller in the state of Florida since 2010. Murphy's Law the popular adage emphasizes anything that goes wrong will go wrong in any giving situation. It is a law from fundamental mentality that is counter-productive deducing the quality and equality of liberty where people live by stating the state orders you to do something by law or there is going to be an intervention of liability against you. There's a harsh draconian fundamental formula in the South I've discerned. I just didn't glance to notice it. I've documented that principle aspect by perception. I payed my rent keeping the peace and permission to live with my family on a contractive basis. This was another atrocity for me. While the shadows of NJ were being dissolved and my life was being remade, I never felt mortified as if someone rewound the old VCR tape to transfix a horror scene, incorporating a new application of fright in a tranquil environment setting. To keep maintained in a needful mind, I restored a hygiene capacity of myself than a sloppy mess, more now, than unprecedented prior when it was 10 years ago as the irony. I'm a natural normal man exasperated from captivity and control, progressive tendencies of critics held against me in an imitating concentration camp of Fascism, where even obedience has forced me roughness on my journey, while, I was in FL from teen years to adulthood. You can take the football player running out of the end zone, but you can't remove the heart out of the captain, the leader or the MVP victor. When my grandmother died July 3rd, 2009 I was lethargic further anguish. I was deeply rooted in family ties with my grandmother. In college I would visit her take care of her to the best of my ability would permit me to. I would stay closer with her for lunch and keep her company. I would perform dwelling jobs and earn money. After she died, she being the matriarch of the entire family-line, the family partially broke-up, subdivided themselves in distance and negated contacting each other on certain imperative occasions. My grandmother was a witness to my character profile. She saw how I had a good head on my shoulders and was committed to my studies. She recognized how I contributed resources and labor to her when she couldn't perform chores around the house in her weakened condition. She compensated me merit of benefit restitution earned. When she died 3 months after my aunt died May 16th, 2009 the entire family situation encumbered a tragedy. We, meaning my family, had 2 wakes and 2 funerals in NJ. After my aunt and grandmother died the will of serenity in my spirit, of me, rotted after moving back to Florida a year later. I had tenacious plans ahead schedule to attend a community college in FL to acquire my Bachelor's in Graphic Arts or B.S. in Communications. My initial proposed plans had been debunked because of the trouble I was legally in as a first time offender. Proactive circumstances preordained had to be cancelled because of insult to injury. So I never fully enjoyed the grandiose opportunity to resurface back up on my feet to participate cultural activities in my community, clearly with obfuscated priorities. Since 2 members died in our family, slowly and stagnant than the average normal person, I couldn't seem to climb the corporate, but commercial ladder seeing other generations outsmarting my excelled generation's advancement with a degeneration upheaval, which consisted of a demoralized, uneconomical, and personable deterioration post "2008." Had I still stayed in NJ with an A.A. in Computer Science Technology, I would have attended another college campus. I would have engaged tuition assistance programs required paying for college courses on campus and books in covered fees, fines and other expenses as a low income individual. I would have worked, wanted to work, and still engaged to be in the work force. I have an anonymous best friend who is dependable and reliable He is like another brother in addition than my own brother. He realizes as I experience the same burden encumbered there's difficulty he goes through at certain indifferent times. On this earth, on solid ground, whether it's sacred rock of freedom or tyranny, if you are in the wilderness of society mocked or chastised the crooked progressive eye of scrutiny the only requirement that should be provided by blood and light is one massive sincere friend that shares viewpoints eager as a brother. I have other friends in other parts of the U.S. and we talk but it's occasional or rarely because of their personal lives, work, or business affairs. In fact you can validate justified conclusion, with reason, it's best to have more passed close relations that are like blood friend, deciphering like-family oriented friends than a hardened family. If you mention politics or deeply rooted in your relationship with your Godly principles for a case to evade argument in your family, people can be condescending against you argumentatively, than distant relations at any random given setting of instances, because identity of ideology. The defaulted results are criticism and hypocrisy should you know you are being poisoned by the secret inner-circle of your family that force you under controlled fundamental deniability. It's best to stay far away in conversation from a negative reaction of the illness. Stay separated as vacated from those doing the poisoning to be withdrawn, to metabolized against the affection detoxed. In 1994 I took a anti-illicit drug protection program taught by law enforcement. I executed all the studies of the program exhibited to pervade resistance against the dangers and adversities of the warranted misuse drug wars with major self-esteem as a kid. Now as an adult what I was educated and taught seems useless and counter-recessive laid passive as forced psychotropic medicines are injected in me forgetting the pointers. I was instilled to pervade for vivid clear conscience. When I was 10 or 11 years old, I swore I would never commit any drug abuse, but as an adult I am placed on psychotropic psychiatric drugs for a disorder diagnosis. However the history pattern of my behavior, my arrests, my dilemmas of unpleasant troubles until rehabilitation, my records were documented over 1/3d my life by a government consumer reporting agency. You know the longer you are on stable psychotropic medicines for a varying degree of different people, especially for men, can reduce a man's stamina, his hygiene imbalanced, his intelligence compromised his nervous system incapacitated impotent acting as an inexpert. His skills, tools, techniques will be substandard from effectively working naturally throughout the years progressing. A man's masculinity will be hampered from growing. A boy won't be able to develop into a man being kept held back. This subtle poison affect destabilizes stagnant the Serotonin and Epinephrine levels to range of competence. What about cellular breakdown which is age acceleration? Inflexibility does more harm than good by subverting harmful chemicals into the brain that are unnatural, abnormal, causing early deaths coped because of a 934.8 billion dollar 5.8% pharmaceutical industry updated since pinpointed 2017. But natural remedies for restoration are either illegal by federal offense or prohibited for cures, or these cures are not disclosed. The American patient treatment holocaust of big Pharma would be closed. I would not be shocked or be a stunningly surprised if some of my stem cells were damaged permanent, because of the forced control of psychotropic medicines institution clinics mandated me to be on a permanent basis, ordering me for years has caused physical damage to my body. I was examined by a professional chiropractor expert, who had a showcase table of his business displayed at my local youth center one day, confessing his determination my nerve ending cords were practically broken and requires reconnection. I can't outtalk my way out of my inescapable fate. When I was previously in FL I was being put to the test here under the gravity of psychological rehabilitation, controlled against liberty and freedoms against my own will as a psychological priority. If you have freedom of speech, and freedom of choice, you should consequently have freedom of wellness. People control you because they want to rent space in your head for monetary gain. It's like the motto-modeled as our military are sworn to serve the national guard after completing 90 days of military training emphatically ***"I take this obligation freely without any mental reservation or purpose of evasion."*** Don't evade someone's mind with any fundamental error through statist control by persuading them with psychotropic medicines *"sweet talking"* is necessary for their condition, stabilizing them when considerably other natural safer ways, alternative medicine to cure a disorder shrinking Pharma when it's not justifiable means. ***"My body, my choice,"*** says the Liberal woman, right? Well what about Conservative rights? What about American morals? Do all Americans have equality too? Do we have to conform only to the unorthodox ideology of progressivism; or, is there a foreshadowed resolution? Both men and women, inconsequent political affiliation, are united. ***"My mind, our freedoms,"*** says the American patriot." I attended therapy for all my total discord embarked sessions with different application discussions of various topics covered each ever-other 2 weeks. I requested therapy, but it was demanded by my family I speak to a counselor. Yet, I feel I couldn't break away of the facilitated position of institutionalism. What was proposed was to further dislodge of my insight for manhood, stripping away the testosterone of my maturity while nurse practitioners and behavior health providers further excoriated me my progress documented in their electronic records of my updated evaluation reported with the state. I had a job in New Jersey before I attended Jr. college. I held a job at a NJ grocery store in the NonFoods department. Once I met a girl who kindly asked me out. She had a dark side to herself. She was strange, but her ideas turned me foolish. I was wise convinced to distrust her to outplay her deception. She used me as a diversion to confront her boyfriend jealous, that she failed to bring into conversation when I met her, stated in the pertinent introduction. Well she did me a favor. I was 21. She was 17 and a minor. She was jail bate. She was under 18 by law. I prevented a crime of statutory rape from happening against dating a minor. I learned my lesson and prevented a legal atrocity from manifesting, knowing then and there, I was being protected by holy forces. Her boyfriend called me and harassed me, but he did me a favor. I called him back attempted to convince him she used me to get him jealous, that I was being setup as a decoy puppet. So that phase in my life ended quietly having limited impact on my work ability and the light grew brighter before I started the semester at college September 2004 in the Computer Animation general applied arts program. That period also terminated the point in my life of my occupation position as a NonFoods Clerk. The store was going to fire me for poor work performance, but I chose to resign for recognition of a clean work record. The conclusion was distress from that girl and lead to breaking a window in the apartment at time the family and I were living in. I had to be stabilized. Attending my 5th or 6th year in college, I had a steady relationship. The girl I dated was naive and wanted to settle down. I wasn't indulged by her offer. I judged to finish college aspiring other important opportunities. She was often sexual active because we were both young, but I sustained control of my sexuality. I resisted prohibiting to go those extra miles of intercourse because I wasn't ready to become a father being without a full-time job, still present in college prior to graduation as a successful certified professional in a career-field before making lucrative pay. Our uncommitted relationship lasted about 3 months, then I decided to break the relationship for an ocean of reasons. While in college I worked at another grocery store for 3 years until March 2008 making excellent pay. I worked 2 part-time jobs before a fast-food restaurant, then it was off to FL which would begin the long unawakened disappointment of atrocity. To state the least case definitively, because of forced med-management I have been rejected free and state expression of input assertion to project any necessary ascertained idea forward where my inherent circumstance couldn't withdraw from institutionalism. I was restricted to testify any case of my permanent circumstance to resonate my story. I was trapped absurd compliance from clinicians to govern my position of having equal liberty, and unescaped control of antiquated warranted psychiatric warfare.

CHAPTER 2

HOLLYWOOD ASPIRATIONS

Subsequent before moving back to Naples, Florida in college I performed 12 plays. I was building up a resume' for Theatre Arts. I had future entertainment aspirations to collect experience for acting development and performance techniques, because I told the guidance counselors I wanted to grow to become an actor in the film industry. They said only the 1% make it because I'm only the 2%. I told critics no matter what, I still intended to pursue this criteria, advancing in this field. Though at college my major was Computer Animation, I had a subtle secondary additional field persuasion for building credit opportunity in the theatrics with plays. I do declare had I not performed in 4 major plays and 8, 2-part summer series of plays total in theatre, I would have not graduated May 2010. I would have graduated 2006 because Jr. college is a 2 years college, but by now it must be a 4 years campus. Plays slowed me down, but engineered the actor's vehicle for me filling my resume. I had the repertoire not to be afraid when I do film because

I had the tools and experience educated when ready to be on the set. But it wasn't quantity of experience, it was quality of networking too. I was not a SAG union member in the industry connecting with the right people at the wrong time; therefrom, I and my family moved back to Naples, FL. I got held back classes exempt dilemma from my family, but a fickle of loyally finishing class requirements in my profession isolated classes particularly related to my major. I was determined to fatten the density pressure of an actor's resume'. I got professional headshots. They were expensive headshots too. The photo center cost me $250-$300.00 for 20 images. So I got the pictures, but never used them or provided use to them uselessly, but casting directors told me they were black and white and had to be in only in color wanting a head-shot with the full aspects of the body in the front and criteria of actor's business card of record of feasible work resume' on the back of the image. Headshots were often expensive subjecting unrealistic prices as $500.00 you pay New York prices. I had to take my own photos labeled unworthy, defamed by casting directors because of mess and sloppiness obfuscated resolution content. I had to get an education. Further subsequent resources were necessary to acquire idea of the facts about the industry. I subscribed to a popular theatre company magazine. The material referred me incredible documented listings of casting calls, character breakdowns, pay, types of productions, projects, benefits and enlightenment on actor techniques. But because most projects were either New York or California, I was moving back to Naples. I cancelled my subscription. I had the Eastside title issue. Not only did I cancel my order, I stipulated the catalyst disorder on my dream, which caused me to display emotional disheartenment unexpressed, but dormant. I was dissatisfied of the apparent situation, even the aftermath of my accidental incidences after moving back to FL. I couldn't processes the subject even if my family were all in ultimatum agreement. Periodically when I was there, I would be either get legit or ill-legitimate calls from 3rd party casting directors from all across the USA. My mom would shut them out, hang up on them and tell them not to call them again. I would feel impacted remorsefully that skepticism of my acting credibility and ingenuity chances of advancement, would be blocked, because my mom always had to be overprotective of my career path for my safety. She would always lecture me about scams and deceptions. She was right. Never sign a terms and conditions contract unobserved, until you don't know what incontrovertible rule, pointer, or statement will survive the paragraph of contract once you authorize a contract. Never relinquish money up front for advancement pay before a job is completed. Once you do, reason is, because you are locked into a partnership of friendliness for business on good terms you can't be outsmarted a bad move decision of being duped by deceivers. Never promise to give money upfront for a business without a prosperous interview, audition or conference because of persistent conned scamming in the industry. Industry is suppose to operate on a contingent basis. The result is liability and you'll cope never seeing that security you saved hard work for a job or life savings again from something important. You meet a film crew on good terms then leave with a record of incredible terms what you received. Judge wisely, judge often as you can with sensible alertness. But when a talent industry was legit, professional casting directors contacted us at our home. I thought this was a milestone breakthrough for me. I assumed foolishly I can fit-in like other individuals who were underprivileged unlike me that has an evident long-list of experienced work condoned with plays and classes taught from college in my community that educated me from scene study, dynamic movement, accent reduction, vocal production and character development. I have a strict family. As previously stated in this book, I couldn't have preference to grow. That encumbered an impractical chance to expand maturity complicated beyond the horizon of the sun. I traveled to New York a couple of times for auditions having 1 acting job according to network correspondence through my family's relations at the time. I'm the 98% of 2% not the 99.9% of 1% reiterated. When I would mention the subject of casting calls of classes for acting, whether it was New York or local, for film or stage, the situation was argued on characteristics of money, travel, time, scheduling, and availability. I would feel resented, restrained from ridicule after the following was said in the family: ***"Don't look at me I don't have any money, you're on your own. You have a brother to pick up from school to care for."*** The authenticity of facts were indescribable insecurity, but accurate. My brother was young and a priority to look after from birth to young teen years, which was a negated element to my acting path before moving back to FL; and, being away from showbiz areas. Apparently I was interlocked into an inescapable destiny I could not return back to my pursuit of happiness, that I studied for at the time chasing only the wind. Between the indifferent confusion of whether I would ingrain my dream of being an actor or continue my role of being a permanent babysitter, I managed to keep the world on my shoulders with a facetious disposition like Atlas did according to Greek Mythology. I had a TV job back in 2009 which was a spoof of informercials the TV network, cast, crew and production names are anonymous. But I enjoyed the job. I got benefits of lunch, got paid some money and credit on a resume'. From that point onward, I thought that way ahead, that checkpoint for something that was an excellent groundbreaking development beginning mark. I presumed that job would launch me into a constant profession I could make a permanent career into, but at that time the place we lived at our rent increased. Never assume. Living arrangement conditions changed to be exercised modestly. I had to get a job that required hard labor and talent alone with an acting dream meagerly wasn't going to pay the bills. The family demanded I work, whether it was part-time or full-time. My undivided attention was demanded requiring my position to help raise my brother. My brother's father walked out on him at an early age, so I had to be like a surrogate dad, although, I am his brother. I tirelessly tried to tested the cold waters of my career path, the output aspect of my goals were muddy and lukewarm. I had difficulty with keeping up with my abilities. Talent scouts and casting directors told me I had to sharpen my artistry with more classes. But it wasn't classes that pulled me in reverse behind believing instead of the ahead, it was my inability ineptness to network with agencies in close relations that staggered my placement. I also got required to maneuver possibility of enhancing my skills with acting with local classes in Glen Rock, NJ every week for a day which was $20.00. I inputed as much information necessary as needed on my resume'. Artists supervised lectures of the same typified skills and abilities in theatre monologues, scene study, dynamic movement, audition techniques, accent reduction, vocal production and breaking the 4th wall method techniques in performances, but foretold in a different version barriers. I benefited from the classes. I learned the Meisner Technique. Because of the captivity of being confined to raising a brother compounded my inundated travel to New York for classes and auditions. I wanted to advance. I dreamed of going the extra mile. 9-10 years afterwards was an afterthought of going back to the profession. Sufficing the dream didn't settle the finance bills, didn't put food on the table, and didn't pay rent. Florida isn't exactly the spotlight drama for active performers and talented artists with a history of repeated offenses, society derogatorily stereotypes bad omens of a transfixed counter-productive culture, much different from up North, but imbalanced than the progressive West coast. In relationship to the pagan criminality of drugs, molestation crimes, aggressive miscarried behavior, progressive hatred, and vindictive adversity of pitiful celebrity outcasts consistently in the news 24/7 evasive stories that are imperative from knowing or reading about to the average working class tax-paying American, being in Florida reflected some practiced-patience for reserved-reward earned. I've awakened to actual realization to disassociate from a career in entertainment that would drag me down towards condemnation and rise salvation. Should I had advanced in an advent career that you can't wait for, you have to go after it, there would have been corruptive consequences later on for the record as I got older. I didn't need to be demoralized with instrumental etiquette I was raised with morals. Manners don't protect you against animosity provoking of public anarchy. My troubled incidences in Naples, FL saved my life, than justifiably leaving a digital footprint record of being a nuisance at the matter of times I finished writing my unsuccessful 1st backstory superhero novel *"The Blue Sphere."* So the irony dictated a career to became an literary author than an actor. Unimaginable Psychiatry recommendations were forced on me without the representation of my acknowledged decision of justice alone. I known my mind and analyzed myself recording chemistry level changes, determining the psychotropic anti-depressant drugs decreased HIC blood-level hemoglobin testosterone levels left in disrepair. This reaction curtailed me to returning back in the public eye as an artist to the industry sluggish than usual. Suppressant limitations were generating my ability coherently to date or get married, to have a courtship with a woman and to have my own family to descend the timeline of my family tree. Resisting to reenter the entertainment force means you have to be part of a union. I'm not part of a union. Unions judge the case of criteria preference of finances when you get paid, how much are withheld for taxes, when you get benefits and tax revenue changes in your 1099/1040. Being a famous celebrity translates you have the paparazzi following you, writing falsified stories of scandal and controversy in the tabloids behind your back unverified and non-conformed decadent to the decency of your respect for the rest of your life throughout the world. There's more of a suppressive engine of criminal proceedings from scandal and controversial conspiracy if you become star than unheard from someone of the naked ear. So stay incognito, stay silent often to omit being branded into dirty Godless scandals. Keep your pants and shirt cleaned and on at all times to someone unfamiliar. Keep your shoes tied and your chin high smiling while you walk away unspeaking what actually happens without taking and giving questions, or, you'll wind up in a court of law from some tramp framing after you accused by argumentative slander. So I vividly did my research, gained a spine, and developed a backbone. The window of sanity decompressed off my shoulders when gossip of the garbage rotted that entity of entertainment, year after year, decade for the decade and desecrated the liberty to enter this field for good projects to act upon. That window unsealed opened. I felt light entered the greenhouse of my mind, enlightening me. I felt an expectation of mental seedlings springing wisdom, turning me more intelligent, inclining me smarter, protecting me, fortifying me invulnerable from forewarned opportunities and forbidden trenches, harnessing a scintilla of brightness to stay connected to reason as a commoner to keep suitably stable. I experienced an inner-light in me reserved from the unworthy imbalance of the progressive agenda, to be more of a delightful person, to withstand the selfish indulgence of absolute fame, power, and fortune, not impeding on meditating a clear conscience and sound head. Abstaining from the pride of corruption was the application logic of authentic artistry for me over unrealistic incompetence, proving rightful choices judges a controlling chance to benefit humility. I could equate daily standards uncomplicated and impact expedient disposal of defiant dishonesty from degenerating elitism obstructing me. Once in Spring or Summer of 2009 I attended an academy of dramatic arts. I met a famous instructor in a scene study project. We had a discussion and he complimented me, addressing how I would fit perfect in the role. He expressed his opinion that I resembled a character from the book adaptation of that's a drama I match the character description criteria. I thanked him for his kindness, his service gratitude opportunity of interviewing me, but the interview was short. What was offered had been denied. It was to get in the academy by best performance inaugurated, delivered quality appeal of character and accuracy. I didn't qualify. Only the 1% handful 1,000s of people per-year who auditioned was quite a bit challenging, admittedly for outsiders and those that lived in the NYC subregion that went to film school, or, some entity of performing arts in their college years were eligible. I only had 1/2 an hour of talk time with the instructor from of a 5 hour complimentary class that shown a list of provided expensive programs they offered. I had to rush to return to bus station at Port Authority. I'll never forget his supporting compliment. It was strong encouragement to return back to the city and reattempt to audition. I couldn't afford trips between the city and home, and once I moved back to FL my acting days of adventure would end by consideration of the family. However as adjacent years passed for me, subsequent, the industry dwindled decadent. My provided wisdom surrogate instructed me with clarity. Better grasp of understanding urged me to remain invisible of an irrecuperable business. Getting into the film and theatre companies was the spinning wheel of chance playing a TV game show for me. The mental arrow kept landing on bankrupt instead to point a form of lieu to win some money, or, hansom reward of benefit for the trial of error to divert the difficult ways. I deserved justification. I wanted to endeavor nobility by tasting a piece of the showbiz pie. I wasn't the square root sum of belonging to the same group of fake celebrities that pretend all their lives. No, in my shoes I was still the common denominator eliminated from the field of probable bright light of answers that still maintained some form of control restrained disestablishment captivity from exploiting my talents in showbiz. I was just a pestered little boy, immune from maturity from his family, at home, echoing a disadvantage to pervade the same envied possibilities seen, heard, and sensed from entertainers a lifetime. Frequently I had to update my theatrical resume.' I took a actors' resume' 101 skills session from and instructor. She said that if I want to excel and advance massively in this industry, not only do I need credentials, I need to network limiting my capacity of intellectual redundancy. I needed insight. Be observant, take notes, listen and speak intelligently when rehearsing your lines in action; perform the best of your ability staying close attention in sight to detail, and most of all inquire to imply statements particular relevant to acting that will brush-up your experience as an artist. Apply realism in your character development to when you stay in character. So it was no crime to find adequate skills for additional help strengthening my acting tools, getting key-pointers on an actor's foundation, and affordable resources that can assist me decisions to networking outstanding jobs. I did, but also could not afford classes in the city. It was strictly forbidden. This was the last visit to Manhattan, walking blocks of exhaustion just to find my teacher, getting nothing in return only advice from word of mouth and an empty wallet. I payed the instructor a check of $100.00 dollars for the day and that was the last I ever saw of her. She critiqued my resume and headshot. It was obfuscated faded unclean and unnecessary too much information as needed. My headshot wasn't quite good quality because it was based of home job images. The image was poor. She said that should I advance to the next staged level of my career, full body shots or head shots 5x9 or 8.5x11 images, color preference than black and white and resume' 1-side of work experience was required. That's the idea. I learned something new. It stuck to me like glue, but knew, I could never use to my benefit for another project now that my destiny lied due South for Florida, returned to Naples, retracing shadows to where my upbringing roots were planted as a teenager. The instructor also implied I limited tools of skills for selling myself as an actor, therefore legit, I staggered substance. In fact someone spotlighted my character reference for a career profession and insulted my dignity by stating: ***"I'm a doer not an achiever; only a starter not a finisher."*** To brush-up my personal limited lack of inexperience. I started developing my home-job Youtube talent audition tapes. I practiced my own version of reenacted scenes from great films with dramatic shots with hopes faithfully I would get noticed to develop faithful substance loyal to managing my goals. I did, but not by industry talent scouts or representatives, but regular average posters on a regular basis provided me some attention. There were essentially comments and statements that were criticizing and harassing, than homaged tribute. I know, I believe (opinion) was sensationally outstanding. I was expanding essential instead of becoming expendable density of my skills to grow. What I did to get out of becoming a partial filmmaker transitory was inspire to collect benefit for credit that would impact my coordination achieving as a beginner performer. As time pondered, I was outbraving the tempest of the sea, sailing the ship over the clashing waves of doom to get to land. I had an imagination for fantasy, drama, and action to act in art and media. I had a gift for creativity of being a creator and generating ideas, being dynamic and versatile. No one in the industry would take a poor tax payer commonwealth American seriously with natural God-given equipment the Lord provided me. I even digitalized, rendered, and animated cartoons from the effective knowledge I adapted in Jr. college. One day my mom received a call from a talent agency recruiter out in Los Angeles, CA. Agents must of inspected carefully my work and were interested in wanting to meet me for a screen-test for a film project out west. However unfortunately I griped at that time. I didn't have talent management. No agency would represent me as an agent. I resisted from the casting call audition to be forgotten. I was thrown under the bus in a rerun. It was another rejection for another opportunity that knocked on the door or rang the door bell. I was disheartened because someone saw my rendered cartoons online and wanted to interview me for a job, because I'm talent material. I was held back in confidence from the cruelty of parental subordination. I didn't give up by that time I had been already settled in Florida. I was still prevalent in subtle dramatic projects that were connected with entertainment. It wasn't soon enough coincidental, at that time, I would persevere to change my affiliate career-title from actor to author. I performed practiced voice-overs from cartoons to movies of famous actors. I even did a demo tape and took a voice-over demo class in Fair Lawn, NJ that I listed diverse separate on my actor's resume' for referenced work. I was spectacular. However, my performance was inessential to the public eye to be chastised by my family. I felt the cold shiver of socialized progressive attacks silencing my happiness of free expression. I was blunt conscience of resentment from others judged thoughts of subconscious imagination affairs, keeping my talents suppressed incapacitated, obstructed from sharing my capabilities exercised with an acting recruiter talent scout, while my dreams were being kidnapped from my attention. Criticism was engineering a spark behind my mind. It was a silent coup of a parental manifesto indecisive trapped against my position because bills in the dwelling compiled, the scarceness of food present and yelling from my family of unplanned action motioned to move forward When I returned to NJ, I must of attended 5, 6 maybe 7 acting classes in and out of NYC being in 2 or 3 of them. But the quality of superior details still remained sustained until 10 years later I feathered remembrance of what was taught to me. The knowledge of classes were informative with the experiences, but to develop into the actual business would integrate useless. My heart was urging to travel in the right place at a time the sun dawned rising on the entertainment spotlight and beforehand years that its soul of the sun would set behind the mountain. I considered the conscientious realism of worldly responsibility to still work full-time. There were conflicts of disinterest forced. I would be required to stipulate charitable donations to profit funds for my family for dwelling expenses which pleasantly changed dynamics of them happier the 8 years we were in NJ countless days. I was enlightened by one of my experienced instructors from one of the classes I took, that when you have a speaking role or doing 1 year's work of a Non-Union film project, you receive your union card in the mail according to procedural standards. As documented earlier, I had a TV job in New York from family relations. I got paid, benefits, lunch, experience on my resume' and a copy demo reel of the completed project to retain. Had there been 1 speaking role doing 1 year's work, I would have been automatically been eligibly enrolled in the union as a viable candidate assigned my first manager to assist me getting acting roles. I would have gotten paid hundreds of thousands of dollars first year starting salary according to contract dealings, not millions grossed yet, but enough to survive by to assist my family. My family kept repeating hysteria arguments of the subject and badgered me, I was living a fantasy and dissuading I live in a delusion world, unconvinced. I moved on turning the pages of the tutorial tool book, but immoveable to deviate my desires. I stayed amicable to the family inflicted with conflict, but was invulnerable from pain of a dwelling war. I would have been material worthy for NY or LA roles becoming thoroughly noticeable, filling up a talent profile or electronic record characterized on Wikipedia. But being hassled as the 98%, the impoverish was a forced requirement not to purposely break the financial bubble of self-sufficiency unless authorized. The treatment I got from family apathy is like flying coach on a commercial airliner, while they would fly first class extravagant from my achievements in conscious active imagination. Meanwhile as we got back to Naples July 11th, 2010 I researched theatre companies downtown. There was a local theatre company in Naples. I went on interview having a few thunderous auditions. I never actually auditioned for a dance and song number recital theatre company production that required steps for a dance and vocal piece evoked, not in even for a piece I done. During my meeting at the audition with casting directors at a local Naples theatre company, I met their senior director. She gave me free-of-charge advice and detailed that I'm talented. She even spoke that I could do anything I set my mind on, incorporate my heart to as a plan. She said, *"you're good at reciting lines and we're happy to have met you, but we receive so many people's resumes who audition per year for productions we eliminate only a few handful of people who are eligibly approved or denied into our theatre company."* As an individual she persuaded me to change my mind, and she was encouraging. She told me to keep inspiring momentum not to quit early. Castings were a competition. I was a grain seed up against the wind. My back was up against the wall. I felt I kept blowing back from the wind as the farmer was reaching forward to snag me from the dirt so he would plant me elsewhere, and I would grow into a tree to be fruitful with abilities, that neither never an outspoken matter of importance what was implied independent drama and action is dependent on tangible results for clear palpable vision to journey. What I contained was a limited inability to produce achievement. Being out of the spotlight from the city and in the South for over a decade curtailed hope for renewed faith to become transparent of my surreal actor's dream to be restored. 10 years passed. I found myself older. I'm now disabled through the reckoning of passed aggression from others' derogatory control and indescribable discourse of crusade, feuding pugnacious contentment, that, I could not outtalk my way out of senseless disputed attacks. I was crippled, injured and partially immobile mentally from the subverted aggression put on me through a dwelling insurgency for decades, hostile vitriol that has unaccountably stayed unresolved. Through consistent phases from one instance of instigation to another occasionally, I would continue to get outbursts of resentment and criticism, nonstop Fascist-like practices of misconduct in the dwelling, the criminal minds against the front-lines of warfare insurgency that are the letdowns, putdowns, and disappointments rose. If I disclosed politics, subject material thought that constitutes a principle relationship of Conservatism, I would be subjected to object challenges to change the topic of conversation. I would be controlled captive in dwelling overruled objection not to have liberty to express my opinionated ideas smashed as an intellectual American, but have to be represented a disadvantage from the co-dependence of being supported re-correction of facts. There have been scenarios of incessant unjust mistreatment of me being trapped in Communist-designed settings, surrounded by others' progressive attitudes, compressing my beliefs judged what I would remark. I had often thought to relocate better housing arrangements to find affordable places to live, so a foundation of optimism would profess opportunity for me to reengage back in the labor work force, earning a paycheck again. The permanent disability I sustained is an irreversible injury to be reinstated. I cannot relocate without due to a fixed income of checks and balances of more than I can spend and save per month. Should I ever decide to relocate, unless inherit wealth of resources, because of my debilitated disorder I would need voluntary permanent case management supplemental to make that possible reality function for the crippled position of my psychological profile.

CHAPTER 3

BEST SELLER BOOKS

On February 2004, in the month of love and devotion, I was getting out of my old 1996 Pontiac SunFire in Elmwood Park, NJ, by my local grocery store. I was going to inquire about a part-time job for a steady paycheck and continual work filling out all the proper forms, W4 tax documents, background checks, drug screening, and job interview. I landed a job in the NonFoods department which lasted only 8 months, at that time concurring, I attended my 1st year of Jr. college. The pointers and factors I'm regurgitating wasn't the job. At that revelation it was the starting initial point I would get the epiphany for what would be my first book idea to my new superhero invention *"The Blue Sphere."* I didn't start writing the backstory until 2010 after I graduated Jr. college. I didn't anticipate immoderately a successful story of an epic adventure and new creativity wouldn't sell to the mindless and rotted millennial generation, who self-serves themselves than pleasing others instead of impartial good of grace for God and unity. So I had an idea for an invention to create a new superhero in the genre that I could benefit from, that what I develop with the tools of my hands could transform me into a public icon. Unfortunately through the incident messes of living in Florida my invention backfired. The popularity interest to search for the story was dead, but what I'm going to do is revolutionize it one day rewritten and revised with a professional editor with recommendations how I can get it to sell to young audiences who would be inspired by an incredible figure in the generation. My book was that required antidote the world needed, that perceived it needless, useless, unwanted and redundant curiosity for delight in quality reading material of old school imagination. So I started working tumultuously on the manuscript 2010, writing my ideas down, developing a theme, characters, setting, plot, and premise what kind of archetype story I wanted to foretell in my novel. It took me 4 prolonged years of writing this blockbuster novel. There were distractions and interruptions that prevented me from reinspecting the manuscript from misprint errors. My family and I had to begin the process of settling in our new home in Naples. I was getting sicker because of lunacy gestures and statements I remarked were foolish. I had to be committed to a psychiatric evaluation as a 1st come, 1st server basis not by choice, but mandatory without independent decision. However there were standard conditions I had to meet deadlines. My first book print and publishing goal would be harder to further extended unreachable. The root foundation I dynamically invented would impact a gravity on insult to deepen the injury from job to job, as the money I needed for promotion and publicity advertisement would be sophisticated to collect and save. Community control was the formula equation substandard for socialized restraint on my conduct, rather than, ironic quality work gain of character for improvement. I would get compliments of solidarity extracting substance of celebration. I was labeled with spiritual liability, discouraged and discoursed to go back and reverse the broken goods in the mouth of the book for the enthusiasm of potential readers, who might consider my material entity subjected auspicious by opinions; while others, would remark it unfavorable. I had limited resources that downturned my unrealistic hopes of merging into the celebrity world. I put my boots on the ground like the army national guard, perhaps the marines against the enemy, kept charging forward with glory of God fortifying my strength more forward, that kept trying to stage my reading material for prepared advertisement. Before the cultivation completion of finishing the manuscript, I would spend hours enervated with writing the factors of the story. I would copy, transfer, extract, exchange and recorded accounts of integrated details from rough draft paper to computer into the irrepressible application format working on The Blue Sphere. I admit, I had 1 inflexible disorder that needed an adjustment. I was a workaholic. I would write from 9:00 PM to 2-3 AM in the morning minimizing my hours of therapeutic lost sleep and restlessly tired. Frankly with all the emotion and change of new memories created present in the passed 10 years, it's a vague foggy memory. I don't often think about the subject. But I still remember, because I saved that memory in the back of my mind when there was family rhetoric, conflict, or resentment, that it often appeared. I remember one day making coffee for breakfast and it was a bright sunny morning. My mom said a compliment responding a few days after The Blue Sphere was initially published. I praised her compliment and appreciated her sincerity. That's the encouragement needed; I longed to hear. I've not only designed the front to back interior and exterior jacket to the book, but drawn dozens of character designs to The Blue Sphere to sell my idea to the industry for lucrative achievement. I still own the original rights under copyright protection law to my invention. I have 2 official dated and signified certificates of intellectually property of ownership, should I revoke my rights owned sold to a major corporation going into mergers and acquisitions for a paid check of profit. The concept of the book was 10 years, writing production was 4, so development and finished project of product was established 14 years a long time. The aftermath only left me with 2-3 royalty checks of only $10.00. I often checked my publisher's yearly book sales report. I never did actually get a release copy of the original transcript. I don't have substantiated proof of my taxable royalty checks that were being withheld from my personal right of ownership and an author. My 1st book was held back in captivity and my role of promoting a new superhero to the foundation of the subculture was controlled by insidious opposition that's a malignant underclass 1% competitive competition absent the support of a literary manager. But here is another punchline. When the manuscript to The Blue Sphere was finished, I iterated, I took a job at another local supermarket. I was going into a contract deal agreement with an undisclosed media producer for radio broadcast advertisement. You have to use your discretionary judgment when going about certain arrangements with entity companies because binding contract policy. I had to be meticulous when promoting my upcoming hugh creation. The book had been published by that time, but I was going to advertise my book through a media market basket of digital satellite radio broadcast for commercial enterprise, having a series of prerecorded taped demo infomercials. I gave permission of advertising agencies to use my non-trademarked artworks for The Blue Sphere at a shopping mall in Orlando, FL to endeavor book popularity trafficking sales in book purchases, which was a doomed epicenter of failure, hoping I would have an evident positive functioning attitude of success. The gentleman that wanted to promote my book on media radio confirmed to authorize business with me. I was ready to sign a contract, but didn't. It would cost $700 dollars to finance informercials in installment payments. Corporate Capitalism is like hot plate of breakfast served ready and hot. You pay little principle security for the profit of products and services and gain capital investment by 1% word of mouth promotion physical advertisement appearance using tools of self-esteem and enthusiasm. You profit large gargantuan quarters of lieu royalty to the collective individual's indispensable rights of liberty. I never signed a contract if persistence of resources is forwarded first efficiently expedient and demanding. When I was hired at my neighborhood supermarket, I was amicable with the store manager. I indirectly implied a moderate compromise with him, briefing to him in the interview, my purpose solely as a sandwich maker would be temporary. I only required to earn a paycheck for expenses to pay the charges on the finance plan for the radio contract. My goal desired was to advertise the attention of a marketable and fashionable campaign with my first book I published.

My rights were denied. There had been liability throughout the entire year I worked at the store. I was roped-in with an inescapable fate from corporate on agreement terms, then at that point all reality concerning the expectations to exploit promotion of my book disappeared. My family disregarded my book as the only thing in life that's important, than the job I was hired for, instead of advancing to promote the book. I lost time and business with the radio jockey ineffectively. I was patient, but everyone else saw my backstory superhero novel impracticable and ill-legitimately in considerable prominence for escape to stardom. It seems I was forced into condescending adult work-labor, getting the run-around, forgetting about my career path as an artist by mental insecurity of reservation. My family demonized the hard work unexpectedly at subtle occasions, that I created exceptionally. Having what material I produced, with the talent of my hands and the prowess skills of my thoughts efficient, I incorporated them into my 1st-14 year book project separate; my book career caved-in, then collapsed. The derision had all been disavowed. It dispossessed from me. My foundation of happiness I would earn from my 1st-book career had been robbed through a way of inconsideration. After the book's final verified work-proof certified completion website was finished I did a bulletin webpage project to showcase my book through an electronic flashing advertisement. I created a flashing banner. I completed it with expectation I would get large volumes of internet trafficking to increase popularity of my book advertisement in its entire format entity, faithful, fans would be encouraged and were ready to read something new, original, and brilliant after I marketed with a publishing company. I was stupefied from blunt ignorance instead of resilience of the 1st achievement I produced. According to my ascertained assertion there was a fraud advertisement of my book The Blue Sphere of over 1,000,000 views on social media. Someone convinced me that it was a hoax glitch created by false spam advertisement through the server. I didn't know which invalid or valid truth at that present time was believable. But that anonymous person was overall the smart winner challenging the debate of the advertisement wars, resolving the dispute, because had it really been over 1,000,000 views of advertisements, potential readers would have flocked to purchase my book from retailers. My royalty program funds would have flooded and escalated hundreds to thousands of dollars extracting taxes of royalties kept out of the companies' retainer fees for marketing, storage, print, cleaning, and other utility purpose insurance concerns according to binding contract agreement. How did I feel? Discouraged and disappointed because my invention that took 14 years to create and invent tirelessly backfired. Word of mouth didn't sell its expectation. I did have much radio broadcast airtime with a family show. I was also disgusted with a disguise of pity and envy. I couldn't revolutionize the grandeur of my story anymore better than even-so transparent. I put my heart, blood, tears, spine and sweat in my first fantasy epic novel. It wasn't justified according to industry's expectations of zealous surreal policy, galvanizing audiences' attraction admired. The impact left me polarized. The only thing I excluded to do was spit in the industry's face the way I established things. I refused to conduct myself that way ethically, using my discretion when detrimental situations fell out of place. I slipped into a hole of misfortune.

I had to rise out of fearless situations with enormous faith. I was trapped captive, gradually over a long period of time for personal, mental, financial, and legal rehabilitation sense of commitment to restore my harmony. From the creation of my book project, its initiation production phase stages, and completion conclusion, the envy of condemnation from others was just warming up the wages of sin. I didn't expect to embark subversion from the egos of public opinion to discourse and home egomania. I did, and from complicity that which preluded domestic crimes that I committed in police custody, would leave the destiny of my book career in a fluke. I was stunned frozen sensitive before my competency had to be restored. Unquestionably, I felt my credibility was misbegotten in discontent and anguish from the scam and deception aspect decadence side of the shady business. There was a binding arrogance when opportunity for promotion and publication was ever-so implied in the discharge response of family conversation. I would be demanded to disdain anonymous phone calls from literary agencies using my mental conscience to process a common sense signal for a red flag disclaimer. I would be then condemned with outrage and urgency not to approach any book talent club agency that demands money upfront for eager promotion of my 1st-book under the submitted authority role obedient from my family. I honored my family's request and rejected phone calls as assertive priority with competent distinction. When The Blue Sphere was released August 2012, subsequently confessed, I was hosted on a dozen interviews from a jockey in NY. It was my first heard appearance where I would cement my foot in the shadow of the celebrity world. I was elated, delighted, joyful, and exhilarated. But from the promotional advertisements royalty sales, to my yearly sales report were perpetually underproductive and emphatically overwhelmed my concern in a depression. There was conflict. Condescending critics online contacted me through social media and other forms of blogging communication. I was stereotyped through deconstructive criticism. I reassured adversaries that they weren't my acquaintance and cohort rivals, and weren't my friends of any incoherent presence in any frame of mind; therefore, that disestablishes their following attention with the information to reading the story and understanding of ill-literate material will be restored to The Blue Sphere. I did notice errors and glitches in the aftermath submission of my novel, that were confusing to the average reader. Enjoyable reading was disrupted and the reading material experience was a bump in the road. Had I caught my mistakes early like a fish in the net captured, I would not have been mistreated as thrown under the bus. Then what was summarized had been experienced later in action. The subject of circumstances aggressed worse, with the job I was assigned to work at the grocery story, contrary that time my 1st-book had been published. The job I had to work at was considerably more vital than the imperative promotion of The Blue Sphere undermined the present futile authority advancement induction subjected of further subversion. The job was only to collect the capital I required for book advertisement and marketing planned. I would work at the grocery store for 1 year interlocked into an "at-will" agreement contract with friendship of management and corporate. I was essentially married to the store's desires not mine, relinquishing my dreams. I failed to advance my self-precedence hesitating to use my discretion falling short below corporate cronyism. My liberties what I invented, that I had created was nonsense to the public. I realized what was coming into present fruition to the current scenario was ridiculous. I proactivity worked in the deli department making sandwiches. My priority to do dealing advertisements at a mall in Orlando with an agency had expired, as well, with the agency on radio to do guest spots. Time started to fade for this new prototype superhero invention backstory novel condemned. I was soon unremembered, as I returned to the average working class tax paying citizen. Customers at the store in our department appreciated my company and my cheerful personality. Patrons were pleased by my pleasant character that I sold them through high quality products and services. I decided to let God push me out of a dead end. I was uncertain, but probably unknowledgeable of an apparent situation, that it was my impossible timing to be recognized, because the process of writing was lacking brilliant advancement though progressive ineligibility and the sciences of initial liberal exception. Politics also outsmarted my God-given skills. I had to pick myself up and keep writing nearly with equipped efficient practice prevalent with my next books, abiding ardent quality and eloquent passion. I learned to be selfless not to envy millions of books by famous celebrity artists and authors, the 1% of people in the entertainment industry. I was only an amateur, a beginner, and an idealist that only patented an inquisitive question before a rhetorical answer that kept tangling me instead of choosing to follow the powerful way of conquering a solution. The next couple of books, whether it would be months or years, would be supplemental in a case to enhance a system of strengthening support to work performance, from thought and intelligence, as I built into the paramount story premise-promised fabulously molded together. Writing 1 book is a surreal impact imagination, vicarious to a variety of books if you dwell on the contemplation you are going to be renown name nationally over night. It takes years to build a character resume' as an artist in the drama camera of the public eye according to experience, performance, dynamics, and the genesis network of foreshadowed communication interrelations. There were several ways I went about to promote my 1st-book. But because I was limited resources in a scuffle, I could not be invited advent in guest appearances on anyone's special radar of recorded broadcast station except resources in NY. I wanted to do TV appearances on talk shows about my new superhero innovation, introduced proactively to the comic world. I was trapped in Florida to ever-go beyond to a comic convention or book club that would be worthy as acceptable to be chosen for an eligible conference. Conflict of interest. I reasoned with the top popular book seller stores of NY to approve my book in an introductory letter of submission, leveled with literary facilitators about the present adventure my new hero and characters experience in the story, setting, and the exciting premise I developed. My message was flat. My excuse was bogus of a cut off ear to the drunken head of wackiness. The Blue Sphere was unexceptional for the book reviewer to commission a determination indispensably acceptable to display in all major book outlet showcases accessible for book signings and guest appearances. It said in the letter after careful review of consideration, ***"I was denied."*** I was invisible to the hysterics of media mediocrity, the hypocrites of the adverse cartel, completely blank-blinded of concentration outcasts; as if, I was unidentified from the 1% progressives from another realm. The irony is the edgy moment and energy fit-yarning momentum to return to the talent spotlight, but momentarily settling events for returning to the setting was 1 size unfit too small. It took too long for infamous derogatory of others' technicality to become my blamed scapegoat. I've read books to acquire intelligence of the pointers in commercials. When I lived in NJ going to NY, I had a fantasy I wanted to become a transparent reality. That reality was to transition into commercials and projects, so I could merge, settle, and integrate in the field quicker-skillful as a productive actor in the showbiz settling to gain a wide variety access list of feasible work efficiently done, fattening an obese actor's resume' with on camera productions. Apparently, all I did was complain with a repugnant attitude mesmerizing an imagination modeled example of painting an imagination of being stuck in the middle of an intersection, forming a cross and all streets lead to a dead end. The only way to evacuate captivity with no escape route of all 4-corners is to burrow through the sewers skeptically to save yourself waiting for first responder to airlift you out of the pit. So I would patiently wait on God and God would lift me out of the arena where danger might be lurking. You don't go further down the bottom, because if you do, your feelings will confuse your concentration and conflict becomes your initial attention. Should you sink further downward spiraling uncontrollable deeper in the pit, you'll fall and crash in the hole of darkness. Head toward the top of the pit, or wait for an accessible rope or ladder. That's a sign from an angel. You have to climb and rise out of the fearful dilemma, loyally taking courage, putting on your uniform of strength and surmount the trapped debacle having God as your light. Calibrate your decision-making process with remarkable facts and establish an assessed explicable solution to survive. Your priority is that one-action exercising intelligence to work first, not last, programming instinct. Perform a solution often when in dire-straights from the word of the healer himself, God, equipping practical directions. The Blue Sphere was going to have a comic book continuation, but I required to have extra superior training to produce a marvelous revealing comic book. I had the tools, but the timing, resources, and recruiting support was braked---broken. There were legal ramifications that restricted the project's conclusion to bringing the content's expectation material results to life. The comic book foreshadowing the backstory would have been a recourse supplemental endeavor for The Blue Sphere book resurrected recognition. The comic book would have been a recourse extra arm of support to lift or grab hold of my reputation, not gag the air of disbelief taken out of account from my chances desiring popularity. Remember, The Blue Sphere wasn't just a backstory novel. It's an innovative idea. It's a question mark turned into a product and service intended for guests of commercial entertainment enterprise and business relations. It was a superhero that was invented, but unfavorable to the millennial-elite untaken lightly by their conscientious pride consumed for condemnation. I had a huge hunch, that perhaps, had I proposed the procedure meticulous on building the epic fantasy backstory to The Blue Sphere in another decade of time like the 1980s, as an example or another state or retrospect another time, would I have aspired the aspect to equate liberty of reward and honor as the same conflict of interest liberal celebrities receive in entertainment? Would another indifferent time or place made an actual difference instead of my capacity of writing skills? Perhaps there's a lot of fueling speculation and particular inquisition, which persists effective reason embedded conspicuous to my 1st-story being held controlled captive from counter-conflict of criticism. The answer would be empathy and sympathy detailed in the disclosure of the discovery to my project in another place and time. Yes, I would have been accepted worthy and notable. I would not been captive unpleasant for loss of time, deadlines, and underfunded resource liability destroyed critical being in a better appropriate region where the waves that splash business transaction of career development evolve. I would have been treated sympathetic and legit, than beneath the beltway demonized a nuisance after the correction system. I would have had the whole pie or cake of opportunity to self-serve hidden a secret multi-million dollar prize waiting justified for me instead of a dream, a sham, or illusion distorted. That isn't an intensive sense of I'm capable of focusing critically responsible for myself having the ability to use self-control. I used to dispose disputes, disappointing attacks of offenses were waged against me indefensibly. Sad thing to experience poignant mental abuse. Distasteful mental abuse is that certain element associated with the Industrial Military Complex. President Eisenhower warned America about it in the 1950s in different sectors of the public eye in the social welfare system, people carelessly refuse to conform to fundamental arbitration of a concentrated military ordered dwelling and not to communicate. Individuals that are controlled crash, and those which are in captivity disconnect in a dwelling terror. Today I'm now doing well and moving ahead with a consolation of exceptional anticipation of humility. As I learned from my past, I matured reestablishing myself in my position to keep practicing hope and liberty. I'm writing essays, documents, poems, and project ideas modeled in stories more than I did in the past. After the prior unsuccessful release of The Blue Sphere and its title forgotten incognito now since 2012, in 2016 I released my 2nd book. The 2nd book consisted of a series of psychological cliches', a variety of poetic parable sonnets to rebuild people's insecurities, clear confusion, relax paranoia and discontent called ***SplashBreeze: AngelPoint Path Destiny Collection 500 Psalms and Philosophies Affirmed Goals and Skills Management Tool Book.*** The book is a long title duration, but after 2-legal escapades I crucially endeavored to take upon myself, the conscientious priority to write my handbook as a foundation for my recovery, and to restore my condition at that time in my conscientious situation SplashBreeze restored my discontent. The book is compact fitting in your pocket for the brokenhearted. The best feature of SplashBreeze as a platform is in fact a comport vehicle intended for decompressing areas of universal pain. I now have 2 book anthologies configured on my resume' with more books further in future development. Additional books are approaching and this spotlight autobiography, being an intermediate is an updated report written to the authentic real-life impact predicament shadows preconditions from trauma, trials, disturbance, and shock. I intent to motivate a vehement of encouragement for others, while others are below the barrel than myself and revive self-esteem in the system. They can look upon me as role-player making a difference for readjustment and reconfiguration, not justified as another celebrity who can't be self-disciplined. The entire dwelling barking like a dog towards me in introspection painted an imagination, as if, I was locked in a hostile prison camp. There were elements of war-embraced Fascist torture through non-verbal militant disagreements, argumentative disputes, and irreconcilable judgment of scrutiny. To be blunt, I would often be stereotyped the incapacity to misfire recall to act and understand critical coherence of attackers that rebelled against me. The passed circumstances didn't help the times I wrote my books. In retrospect, I was baffled from dishonor. The socialized behaviors frivolously neglected and suspended me in rejection, which inhibited potential to distribute my God-given talents and projects of products and services, I developed. I was forced behind, and held back by the dictated progressive tendencies implanted to live and let go denounced my hugh first invention, that could have preluded me to bank a thorough pot of lucky happiness suspended. I mostly blamed excuses on the psychotropic therapy, I was forced to be take through ignorant intimidated manipulation by pharmacology assault. I've heard the old conveyed statements implied repeatedly. ***"You're living in a delusion. That isn't a reality. Get your mind out of the clouds. Art and drama theatrics don't pay the bills."*** True to the working class Commonwealth underclass 2% entertainment can be a feeding joke, which I understand. Tangibly, I would have been assigned a reputable talent recruiter had my material contents of work went the extra miles, but flatlined a heart attack. Some implied wisdom: *Secured advocacy would promote introduction of my professional work to ethically encourage businesses for hired potential; therefore, not operate counterproductive insecurity forced against my convenience, because of controlled reluctance mischaracterized indignant.* Fortunately through years of maturity and evolving a backbone spine to manifest integral wisdom through the spirit of God, I had the epiphany calling of revelation to have the appropriate humility to distance myself from a perverse industry. My option to reverse course of vulnerable destruction, prevented years of chaos which would further dwindle my demeanor of practical torment futile.

CHAPTER 4

CRIME AND CONTROL

Time required to adjust transitioning from NJ back to FL didn't seem suitable. I had to rethink my traceable footsteps resetting back to the place where I graduated high school 2002 emphasizing why I had to return to the place I grew up, but years later in unfamiliar territory. I was overwhelmed capitulated with a cold nerve griping pitiful confusion I never suffered the misbegotten toxicity before since returning to Naples, the aftermath of a few weeks would be the expectation ignition of disliking the towns policy of a community control. Circumstances were about to change for the rest of my life after 10 weeks to 2 months, while settling in the new condominium that would take a longer period to relinquish my condition.

The impact of the family assimilating separate on their own was the epicenter trauma that rocked and shocked the breakup of the entire family. It would be the start of division and evasiveness for the impact of my family, archaic emotions binding. I was beginning to feel like Christ how he went into the desert for 40 days and 40 nights without food but water. The indicative model in my position was the untimely prediction of years, I would spend, in the wilderness without food for tradition and drink of culture replaced with barriers and borders from a psychosomatic platform of controlling authority. It was the beginning of an insidious ego by public opinion priority. Animosity was creeping in the deep shadows of darkness from every edgy corner of danger from my family's controlling disdain concerns, to the concerns of others' impertinent misrepresentations of drama, disorganized from the practices divulged the inclined concern of social service benefits of ostentatious financial, health, and legal resources at that forced standpoint. I left the fast-food restaurant giving 2 weeks noticed in NJ. I left on good moral judged terms and conditions resigning after completing a 1 year training period of assessments. The manager was eager of my work ethic and said I was a nobel employee of ardent job performance. My ability to cope and work-well with others was respectful and courteous. I earned a letter of accommodation almost receiving employee of the month. I loved my job showing honor towards my supervising manager. It wouldn't be until 2 weeks afterwards, the aftermath, I would be reemployed for another, but formal restaurant position in Naples as a precook baker. I was a beginner. I only worked for 2 weeks where I was being trained and didn't pay attention to detail. I had frustration to following directions, reading instructions, writing facts and following-through with orders to function my job performance, which is a reason in association to another dilemma a fickle disturbance lead me irreconcilable to a resignation asked. A near life-threatening accident crime occurred at home which made local news connected to the details of breaking information in relationship to my case. Because of my distorted incapacitated condition, I kept withdrawing employment frequently. On September 2nd, 2010 just a little over 2 weeks when I started a new job at a health nutrition restaurant with a bakery, I committed a domestic violent crime at home against my mother. She was okay and alive, but injured. I was arrested for a 3rd degree misdemeanor battery, handcuffed, transported downtown to the sheriff's detention center station and booked on battery charges. This was my 1st offense charge and record in the initial history coverage of my life. I was never a violent man until that 1st obtuse insensitive crime occurred. That reminiscence precedent was a horrible night of terror and stress to begin with shocked in memory. I had just gotten off work hours prior to writing The Blue Sphere manuscript, committed to my first book. I was also in the process of registering my LLC corporate entity. I had to personalize my logo entrepreneur small business. I had a small business logo for embroidery merchandizing with failed negated effort to file a trademark license with commerce the 2010s. That September 2nd, 2010 I misbehaved; I was inappropriate. I won't discuss the nature of my criminal cases in my book even though the cases are closed by law. You can read and review the nature of the records in a background check or personalized criminal history report in public record and in the national data bases with a consumer reporting agency permanent report. Everything today is public record online the internet. I will detail the nature of the crime was horrendous. Had my mother been killed I would have been convicted to prison doing hard time in a Florida state prison a lifetime without parole for an accidental death or received the death penalty. It's a miracle she's a alive that a death had been prevented. I didn't talk about the subjects before, until years later pacified because vehement pressure of discussing my incidences would absorb sensitive criticism from opposition growing snakes of enemies in numbers. I would be outnumbered acquaintances and friends, then I would receive attacks from adversaries. That was also a night in memory disorganized, In those pacified days of my younger adult years, I had limited grip of my emotions, my personality was hardheaded, and a tea kettle always steaming mad. I was angry on a consistent basis, unstable and a controlling force to take psychotropic medication at that time when the crime manifested. I was allergic to a medicine which caused respiratory arrest. I disassociated that irregular content displacement on a rehabilitated replacement. I was in jail for 3 days, and after 3 days, I immediately had a court appearance in front of a court circuit judge from a bench trial. I was seen for 15-20 minute that day on September 5th or the 6th by behavior health administrators, social workers, clinical psychologists and their appointed forensic team for my case. My public defender coached me to enter a plea of *"no contest."* I entered a plea and in the discovery found me not guilty by reason of insanity of the only 3 statues in FL. I refused to fight the charges and accepted my punishment done. I had 1 year probation, a 10 weeks anger management course, and 5 months community service to pay back all comprehensive lieu of court fees I had been mandated to pay according to the judge's orders. I then realized that moment, for a crime I didn't ask, except for having enmity for the incompetent complicity that resulted, I was condemned under the spiritual sedation of authority powers. I was being played for a fool subservient by the authoritarian manifesto spindle-spinning me like a bottle around by my family where the insult of injury would cause permanent wreckage. Spineless misacts would be invulnerable to restore the inevitable damage the organized effort of my authorship occupation performed as a life-long beginning career author. I couldn't earn the resolving peace of relief pacifism deserved because of these predicaments. When the first crime was committed I was handcuffed, doubled locked by sheriff deputies. I was escorted out of the premises and the injured taken to the hospital for medical treatment in intensive care. I was lucky on a razor edge wasn't facing attempted murder charges, fortunate to be protected and safe from the insolent attacks of violence that happened. As soon as I got down the police station I was read my miranda rights, ordered to stay silent until I met with my defense attorney or public defender assigned to my case. The jail food was terrible. Bread, water and meatless main course was served oblivious with no element of texture for distaste. You can almost gag on the food which was served. It was my first offense, begrudged, I still remember on a basis. I had to stay quiet, read books, and follow the guards' orders just getting through the detention stages until my public hearing and meeting the attorney-client procedure requirement privileges of terms and conditions before my trial. My mom showed up for the hearing, bandaged and bruised, but strong-hearted with a fighting spirit still determined to see the charges dropped. If a face is shown you have a case. There's a sentencing. The judge withdrew the case and asked if my mom wanted to to pursue pressing charges. No charges were pressed, but a restraining order was authorized effect for 1 year against me until I completed all my programs, probation, court fees and courted ordered treatment plan was terminated for discharge rehabilitation. I took the indisputable medication as proscribed or my stay in jail would further advance against coping the disadvantage of my liberties. When I was in lockup I noticed all my rights by law and all liberties in custody were sanctioned until the charges were dropped, then my civil liberties would be restored. I remained under silence. There were limitations disestablished, or unexplored options to change my medicines that kept me sicker on the current content drug manifesto. I was further poisoned deficient and my incompetence paralyzed dysfunctional. Psychotropic medicines are the highway policy of progressive fundamentalism by doctor's core foundation. You can't argue your way out of indispensable medical enforcement captivity. The police departments treated my cases not as circumstantial accidents, but disrespected history of repeated offenses. My research moving back to Naples upon senseless scenarios, premature at that time, was challenged. Because of the disunity statist state of controlled institutionalism, in Naples FL, I was refused to express my natural contained gifts of self-control, balance, and capacity independence of reason was overlooked. I was resented from having the liberty to perform self-controlled independent decisions. My normal remedies of righteous foods, meditation, and exercises was outsmarted by a police state attitudes instead of justified one-way pointed sign direction indecision options of taking medications. I would be prohibited to have structure to self-think for myself instead of co-depending others to do the thinking for me, how I read, write, speak and eat for me by putting words in my mouth to determine my character, judging me. I would be an abstract personal character, unauthorized to have a virtue of substance. There were doubts that I couldn't analyze information by breaking down communication, restructuring intelligence arranged in the volume perimeter boundaries of valid reason. Critics would examine my behavior redundant, poor memory, unclear thoughts, and skipped speech patterns that I was ignoring the less is more rule, when I have been conforming to a critical thinking system using an application of common sense. I would be often positioned in a state of mental solitary confinement in by constant community control ordered to take chemical compound pharmaceutical agents produced by the sophisticated intelligence of superior progressivism rejecting my usage of composited skills and formulas of computation overruled. Explanations were not honored and tribute contributed wasn't accepted rather an exemption. We hardly identify people as humans if we forgive the error picking up the broken pieces repairing the damage, but ironically disguise all humans as patients. We call controlled patients tagged criminals under our breath captive in the mischaracterized actions as people respond to an individual indifferently, processed and facilitated, even if they have been rehabilitated. So I had 1 year probation. I reiterate the mentioned description of sentence warranted about at least 1 of the sentences of my treatment plan. I met my probation officer. I had to check in once a month on time at probation for 1 year September 2010-2011. I also had curfew to abide by the rules. I couldn't be under the influence of any paraphernalia non-applicable apparently implied. In 1 year's time I went from a skeptic to optimistic and believably healed. I avoided adverse trouble. But because there was also an ongoing restraining order from my family court ordered, I was mandated to stay 90 days at a community homeless shelter. On specific days I would also be required to attend a career resource center to look for active gainful employment, resume' building and interview skills development searching diligently for a job. I had to pay $50 dollars per week for room and board rent. First 2 weeks were free. I was disheartened I couldn't see my family, but obedience of independence self-taught me to be responsible, a sense of maturity and obligation to be skillfully taken care of responsibilities for myself during the situation to be independent coping support from case management. I would volunteer in the soup kitchen frequently offering to provide contribution of my free time to cook gourmet food for the homeless shelter, which was working credit towards my rent and program fees. I was assigned a case manager that instructed me to write down my short-term and long-term goals. My case manager also encouraged me to persist actively work towards recovery and seek employment. Dinner was served at 5:00 PM. Our finances paid for our meals. Residents would be assigned a janitorial chore duties designated to perform an assigned chore duty every night. If we refused we'd have a written notice warning that disciplinary action will lead to further consequences by supervised management. 3 written notices you're dismissed from the program. The residents had to breathalyze every night for traces of alcohol and check-in by their probation officer. I felt uncomfortable that I didn't fit-in into the environment. Being in that environment around addicts where consciously forced in that setting, that have a serious platform of disorders, were far worse than the clean position, that I was, and far unfamiliar with in my expertise. I was blocked from contacting my family by police restriction. I felt stereotyped like trash and this was around the time when I was a 1st time book author mistreated disingenuous. Then I looked to realize the deceit my family did to me. I was putting the blame on them, when I committed the crime, which I was partly guilty for and was punished. I was like the prophet Job who lost everything, but his faith in God regained empty prominence returned that was found through him in God. It was a matter of time, patience, and justified forgiveness that had me suspended in animation. As recently mentioned subsequent I had a 10-week course of anger management at the behavior health clinic. I completed the course attending all 10-weeks of the course and had to report my progress with the judge of that length of time. I developed tolerance and control of my aggression, my fury and my anger by a foundation of a motto: ***"Say what you mean, mean what you say, don't say or do a mean."*** I grew thoroughly positive and obedient to be reunited with my family after a year, but still had to be forced control manipulation on the medication tolerant which nobody, but me, identifies the content of discontent an adversity. High authority wouldn't reverence my Constitutionalism. After 10 weeks I received my certification of accomplishment of anger management. I wasn't finished with my sentencing penalty period. My treatment plan still consisted of complying to pay back my court fees. I was assigned a job to report to a nearby facility where the disabled attend to participate in daily activities, and visit a place for socializing special services in their local community. I had to perform maintenance services of thorough cleaning for 5-6 months to build points of credit of all warranted lieu returned back to the courts. So from January to June 2011 I completed efficient community service for the first time of my major 1st-offense to the best of my ability would permit me to perform. I returned to court transferring my community service progress report records of work habit points collected for services documented. A year later the judge dropped the charges and the restraining order was removed. The restraining order expired. I saw my family and was allowed to return home after 6 months of community services. But I continued to go on probation paying $75.00 in probation fees while being at home. All my fees, fines, and penalties were paid up to initial date. But I had a circulating permanent record which court and criminal records on the crime data network that I could not debunk, annul, or expunge remained. If I could erase the incriminating history of my declassified record for infamous engagement I would, but I can't, which inflexibility took place. The cost alone would be millions of dollars I'm inconceivable of presenting ownership of insufficient funds to the impossible would take years of work to pay to remove the endless content from disreputable sites paid through webmaster domain owners or chief administrators. After I finished all my legal drama battles, I finally published The Blue Sphere August 2012. The damage had already been done; the attraction bell of dismissal for media-hype of my inventions release had been rung. The devil was in the contract of details. My criminal record, my legal drama, my odyssey for voyaging the impact from experiencing my visit to county jail put a damper for any accountable chance of publicity.

All the drastic frustration to rebuilding momentum for The Blue Sphere mellowed and forced to be forgotten. My sibling said that the structure of writing is misconstrued, unclear, compounding, and unintelligent for competent followers who will lose interest in this type of material I have written which was ill-literate. I was accused of disavowing myself guilty a criminal writer of my own self-made work. The materialism of my character was evidently being misapprehended from those ungratified, who have a narrow idealistic vague opinion of critical effort coping intricate difficulty my skills of me are attempting to produce quality products and services expedient to the entertainment industry. I was hoping by technical labor and a little faithful prayer, the innovation of my 1st book would perpetuate my continual premise situation for distributed opportunity projects to develop. Instead of evolution, the punishment undeserved and unresolved penalty I received at any present unpleasure breath of mercy, would be a technicality aversion of malignant innuendos. I was unprotected. My guard was down. Conflict of interest was a conflict judged of my book ineligible criteria because of favoritism. I have now, than before, rebuilt the moral compass foundation revived of the crippling dilemma I embattled. There was yelling, screaming, and shouting from my family on to me. My face towards my left-eye is partly disfigured of damage from intense boisterous arguing. At random times I would be late for work before I officially was declared disabled in my condition. I was reprimanded by managers in different jobs and documented with a discipline lecture because of the skeptical isolated scenarios that were outplayed at home. I would be maltreated like a demagogue and when I would assist a dwelling-lock repair I would be ridiculed incompetence because my work performance was inefficient. I would take my time stagnantly to ensure the job would be done right efficiently. The crimes that manifested punctually resulted defective errors through evident altercations of abuse and escalated towards violence. There would be profanity, slurs of unapologetic remarks I debunked untrue, and disparaging abuse that I was ashamed. I would sometimes get the impression I was trapped like a mouse, or a bird in a cage about to get eaten because radical insurgency of parental statism in the dwelling, when the domestic crimes went rampant, were becoming apparent. One door closes and another chapter opens, but my book of foretelling petrified captivity that happened was about to get a lot detailing of accountability. I would be blamed accused of being delusional, because I was smart sensing what I was experiencing from the socialized aggression, sandwiched in the middle between the terrors of my family's uneasy debacle on the edge. I so much wanted to date more, filtering the opportunity to meet other people having a steady relationship leading to marriage, but through the years of weariness from the impact of mental abuse, the nightmare resulted in exhaustion and fatigue. I grew older and most of my generation already married to have children of their own, living their own lives differently. Sins were forced upon me as the world compressed their sins on Jesus Christ isolating him to die on the cross before those 3 days expectation of serenity. I knew I was going to survive to tell my story. It would be a matter of estimated time the details would be explored. For a 1st time book author my skills were disbelieved. I however had patience having hope and joy. I sustained my attitude of selfless self-esteem determination to still be considerable, despite often being dispirited and judged impractical. I would periodically believe in myself, my father would be proud of me being a 2-time book author with more books developed ahead for aspired achievement. I worked, wrote, critiqued and revised every square inch criteria of conscientious material. The court of public opinion zeroing-in the sheriff deputized mind of the individual world would remain unsustainably adamant to change their decision for transparent content, content that communicates advent instead of pushing apathetic enemies away from their egregious position. After a few years passed things seemed to be okay, but I would be demanded community control by consistent psychiatric visits of clinical study. That's Liberal control. That didn't constitute controlling me in a psychotropic setting phenomenon consumed. At the present time of December 2013-January 2015 I had been working at another local grocery store for 1 year. Things seemed to be going suitable for awhile. I had a plan to stay for a year and earn an accomplishment valued employee award the longer I stayed for good ethic of work. I didn't fit-in to the atmosphere. I did my job according to company policy. I was reprimanded for misconducted twice that were untrue. According to management I performed poorly than my computerized tested, that I staggered to finish before the year had been terminated as a Premium Deli Specialist Sandwich Maker. Then oblivious planning flawed to be what next inconspicuous fickle occurred. I was called for a conference into the general manager's office. I was being watched from the operating surveillance camera. There were 3 sheriff deputies waiting in the manager's office for me. The manager commented a statement that we are terminating your partnership with the store, after I told him months prior when I was hired I was a pacifist. The 3 sheriff deputies escorted me out of the store with a no trespass order not to loiter 50 feet of the store or I'll be arrested against my civil liberties. This drastic element was 2015 when the overwhelming legal episode of drama took place. I then contacted corporate if I'm ever eligible for rehire for employment for the store. I'm on a suspension list to ever apply for the grocery store again indefinitely; unless, I file an appeal with corporate for a certain length of time because of my record of leaving on bad terms. I put in an appeal which is up to 5 years before determination can be approved to incorporate a completed employment application with the grocery store. 2015 was going to be a year of ambiance and trouble for me. I had 2 baker acts in the state of FL. I caused a ruckus at home and a legal intervention notified police authorities to confront me baker acted in custody for evaluation precaution in our town's behavior health clinic, involuntarily confined me as an impatient in the intake unit for public general safety, that I wasn't a danger to myself and others around me. I was held accountable for what I didn't do, say, or understand against my Constitutional rights being infringed upon. I must of said an awkward statement that landed me in to be disciplined in hot water. Staff showed urgent concern that I had be baker acted again. I never spoke any threats that defamatory, but a positive remark towards care towards my fellow man showing patriotism, but they still were concerned for safety and had me controlled captive on the unit for 2 weeks. Under observation, my statements spoken to practitioners were consideration of lunacy characteristics from my opinion.

Because of these impetuous baker acts as a priority against my situations, it cost me my job and expensive costs of involuntary stays on the crisis unit. The grocery store wasn't going to keep extending my absents with excuses. It would be a matter of time until they would terminate my partnership with the company since the start of my initial *"at-will"* agreement, with them, December 2013. I had to comply to contribute random paraphernalia screenings because of my behavior, with no presences of narcotics in my neurological system from the statist aspect of institutionalism. Once you're in the correctional system you conform to all perimeters of subordination. The theme of psychology dramatics is nearly impossible to get out with the proxy shadows of governmental abuse following you by force unforgiving and not forgetting. I didn't have heath insurance prevalent, at that time, so I had to pay over $167 dollars for involuntary treatment care trapped in a behavior health facility clinic patient unit from about 2 weeks estimated for food, bedding, medical treatment and redundant recovery recommended. I would still be forced to be med-compliant. I got out voluntarily backer act as an intake, but lost much employment opportunities. I lost days of available accountability pay and work days being trapped in a patient intake medical unit because of a falsified stereotyped reaction to my response on my behavior that was mishandled. Another immoral crime ultimatum was about to strike further control captive a fiasco upon my Constitutional independence, manhandling me a discrepancy inviolate, where the instance of the diagnosis would be unclear, if I could be ever be allowed to self-govern my inherent liberty free and separate from the psychiatric community of doctors' gripping endless reservation of revolution. I complied and continued to be proscribed anti-psychotic mood stabilizers uncorrelated maniacal. I'm familiar in the griped relationship with understanding balance of my own mind. I never was disturbed, justified to be placed on the interference of psychotropic restraint constricted control as an understatement to elaborate. I have been mischaracterized from a theme of statist Totalitarianism spider's web distribution, from the advanced reckoning contamination of Liberalism, unstoppable and inclined for acceleration generating in a subnormal America.

5

MENTAL HOSPITAL

On October 22nd, 2015 I committed my 2nd offense in my lifetime. I was immature and irresponsible. I got rearrested. I wasn't well. I was mandated to ingest a medicine in the dwelling to be med-compliant or consequences would be thrown out of the condominium. It was either take adverse content or get discharged out of the dwelling, at the same time, I was developing my Philosophy tool book *SplashBreeze AngelPoint Path Destiny Collection 500 Psalm and Philosophy Affirmed Goal and Skills Management Tool Book.* It's a long title, but it was my recovery tool book that would reconcile my condition of my journey back on the road towards restoring my indescribable health and discombobulation of inflexible situations. I was 31 when the 2nd crime occurred and didn't pay any rent to the dwelling for permissible terms and agreement to stay. I remember that day vividly. My plan was to go the library when scheduled an appointment with a psychiatrist unplanned, when I had plans to attend the library and start editing my supporting tool book with spiritual quote excerpts. Also at the same time, that year of events in 2015, was a former commander a chief in office of U.S. politics. From the fundamental corruption that was going on in Washington D.C. in the Administration I was working undercover to get confidential documented reports of his ***secret*** identity deposition, his past dealings with foreign enemies and criminal actions to a watchdog committee for investigating crimes against humanity. I submitted all intelligence to the watchdog agency in government. I had to work quietly incognito for 3 years of material contents provided to the right officials who would accept my records of information in a intelligence report. The report was all valid circumstantial forensic evidence I discovered and examined, but the evidence wasn't tangible facts consistent. My arguments was weak and rejected according to experts at the watchdog council for hearsay theories. I literally was going to save the nation, but instead of having 2 mysterious lives, 1st writing my 2nd book and the other option an intelligence briefing in operation that would have procured charges filed by a subversive justice department on those in a prior administration, my insurance policy to stop a former commander and chief's wrong deception for the supplemental case explored information: I verified, documented, identified, and confirmed would have testified against the impostor of what I saw and his administration to have him and his team indicted, would be only a futile immunity situation. On October 20th, 2015, 2 days before my initial sanctioned arrest, the package material of intelligence report never resonated its daylight of sunrise seen. The nature of my domestic crime at home was a felony detailed in my criminal report, but I was never convicted;

therefore, I'm not a felon on paper just my arrest record is permanent. I was playing vigilante way too overwhelming far inclusive disconnected from actual reality to exaggerate. I didn't use my discretion which was injurious to my legal status. The pain of injury persisted until after my 1-year anniversary being in a jail detention center. All I did, effortlessly, was attempt to save America during a corrupt administration which by them engineered a coup to hold Americans under siege. I didn't identify my boundary limitations of unpleasant trauma. I refused to put a stop to it and the result was I got sanctioned twice being back in FL, from my first arrest when we returned to Naples later of another half decade. Also information was filled out about me in a crime report affidavit with the sheriff's office against me since my first misdemeanor battery charge 2010. I was escorted to the sheriff's office police station down town. This time my stay in jail estimated would be prolonged further for this nature type of crime criteria prohibited. I stayed in jail for 1 year. A no contact order and restraining order was enforced effective from the time I arrived in jail for my indecent action committed at home. I called numerous bail bonds on the pay phone. People that I knew couldn't help me make my bail roughly until my trial and then released on good terms for time served. For my misacts, I didn't deserve to be freed on any set bond. I was beginning question the inevitable if I had been disowned because none of my relatives for nearby bondsman would help my situation if someone would pay $1,000 to pardon me free until my trial. I was abandoned with sinister strangers, hardened criminals and drug offenders where I was placed in an uncomfortable presence of unpleasant circumstances. I spent the holidays

2015 in lockup. I was in a single-cell roughly then assigned a sharing cell in conjunction with other inmates. I was put on the medical step-down holding facility block. I had to follow stifling hardcore tough jail policy rules to avoid secondary charges, because anything I said or did monitored on surveillance would be used against me in a court of law. I was in a cell one-time with a indisputable militant that was trying to convince me to debunk my relationship worship of beliefs, control me, and conform me subnormal fundamentalism to convert my religious identity. I didn't notify the guard, because I didn't want to appear misconceived as a troublemaker with more charges added to my case. I was petrified than having the heart to testify a conscience of courage. I just had to abide by the terms and conditions of the correction system and behave according to my public defender for about 1 year going into 2016, getting through the rough stages of being processed. I was in a cell with a molester that had me shaken paranoid, confused discouraged in shock uncaught by stupefied surprise. I had a breakdown internalized by my spirit, but kept my chin up. I kept hardheaded determined to move forward sprinkling a cliche' pinch of spices of ingredients that required demands of God and his holy spirit cooked by the recipe of faith. My name was announced one day December 2015 for a court appearance by the judge. I was mandated by court order to visit the FL district state hospital in Indian Town. I then also received an prison point check-in sheet document sheet. The courts were in position to determine their verdict ruling to subject me eligible for alleged prison. No, I wasn't convicted. A miracle indicated I had 0-penalty points on my point-card sheet. But by January 20th, 2016 I was transported from the jail to the state behavior health institution. I was handcuffed in shackles; charges were pending. I felt afraid and embarrassed alone away from my family in unknown territory, what was to become apparent of me in a strange place being displaced in another unexpected region of FL. I was to be neurological reprogrammed and restored to the capacity of normal competency level rate of sensible thinking and rational actions, so I could return to court to stand trial and testify applicable on the bench what occurred from the time the crime took place, and why I attacked the victim with an incidental battery. I was found ITP by in the first competency hearing. I arrived at a FL state behavior health forensic institution state hospital that early morning on January 20th, 2016. It was a new year and a beginning of an election year period in politics. Things were ugly for me and cultural changes were revolutionizing in the country, a dismal and dark period in a socialized generation. I was checked-in and registered. I had my vitals taken for examination and the vetting processes of being arranged as a resident for the stay of a 5-month period to raise my competency level so I could stand trial and face my accuser. The victim didn't press charges because she still loved me and didn't want to see me further condemned, just recovered. I conformed to her demands complying with med-management agreement, so it wouldn't constitute being evicted from the condominium, which in my opinion, is realistically an inhumane crime, because I'm part of the family living in the dwelling. She's the owner. I would have justified expanding my living arrangements by paying her rent from the initial beginning of moving back to Naples, facilitating loss time of liability. Returning back to my predicament, being locked away in a state board administrative behavior health hospital, I immediately went on the phone with the operator to get clearance from a branch of government, that would accept my constitutional civil liberties have not been violated. I wanted to make a claim filing and appeal for a pardon. But I had to testify the side of my case having a clear mind of understanding the charges I was facing, why and what happened, when the crime took place to exonerate my innocents. From the turmoil politically and socially that ridiculed our country for 8 years, I was outnumbered. I was unjustified to seek outside resources like a lawyer, or litigation specialist; thereof, funds to afford an attorney for a state judge to drop state criminal charges bringing totality defamation of my character case to a close. I attempted to even contact the justice bureau about my imprisoned circumstance, but no one would listen to my side of the story. I was immobilized helpless; I was reckless since I sent that intelligence report to the watchdog committee that could have questioned a prior administrations concealed valid identity of political dealings through details entailed to his character, that would have impeached him as a sitting impostor, the framework intention of the founding fathers established article II section IV of the Constitution. Several felonies were committed in his administration. According to experts I wasn't well in my right state of mind. Specialists claimed I fabricated the whole criminal story a conspiracy, even though I submitted circumstantial facts instead of physical evidence required on the impostor, but what was necessary wasn't a substantiated blueprint of DNA genetics. However what I was experiencing was cogent and my senses were a strong probable cause, but not convincing enough to inferior cynicism being around insensitive mental health care providers that contained progressive dispositions for my treatment. They didn't care. They didn't support the verified truth present at that time I was proposing. The forensic team thought was just another Schizophrenic decompensated because withdrawal was impacting my behavior health being off the psychotropic agents. I had a bad habit to control functional communication with excessive distention from permanent nervous system wreckage. I had no outside rescue. The state was officially against my case. So I had been admitted in the state hospital. I was baker acted on practical new medicine agent replacements in the 2010s. I was like, *"oh no, now I'm going to go from one agent to another one, but it couldn't be any far worse. Why can't my poor body just be free and clean from all psychotropic pharmaceutical medicines?"* The Pharma-Manifesto escapade factor couldn't endeavor any better, but greater far worse the disloyal sicking side-effects confused consumers disregard paying attention drastically to warning health labels pharmaceutical agencies assign contracts with health care providers, state senior medical agencies, and doctors by licensed prescription therapeutics, providing over the counter drugs label their medical products induced support health-risk related critical information. Even if enough controlled studies of therapy medicines are tested successful on laboratory animals in pain, governments deny natural remedy patent responses efficient from planet cell regeneration research. Contractor lobbyists are dropped the billion's ball forfeited. I have been overworking too much on my books. After the incredible misfortune of The Blue

Sphere's literary demised and close to being a 2nd published book author, my exile was my vacation. It was a safety net contingency than a curse through the probationary correctional system. I needed to recharge my batteries having all the pieces of the broken vase be put back together. I required to be glued to stick and stay whole not falling apart again in a worse case scenario. I had to restore all unquestionable components of my master computer brain. My limited mind then could control creativity as restored my heart, putting greater energy into the passion of my work what I do best, create art through books, writing, and dramatic performance in project ideas. I pocketed recommendations of thoughts in my mind and wrote down scientific ideas for future development of projects I can save coherently without the need of psychotropic medicine. I felt for now my character was going to be permanently disgraced by officials and offenders because of exercising capacity of my original old school thoughts for opinions misconstrued and untaken classic ideas incorporated into practice every time I would speak, or make a suggestion; it would be outclassed judgment with a technicality. But what was ignored was the opposition of liberal progressivism placed and put on me in a stronghold, overwhelmed by forces in a dwelling pushing hostility. I was well cognizant of my surroundings. I was blamed as a lunatic for my actions when my preplanned schedule for projects and work deadlines put me in the spotlight of examination for behavior health inspection, instead ignored justified a normal guy that forfeit his A.A. in Computer Science Technology, former actor on stage, 1 former opportunity on TV, who wanted to make it big in the hurricane eye of the entertainment spectrum for showbiz earning popular reward was deserving. I stayed at the hospital viably with a fervent attitude, so I wouldn't wind up locked in my room. I kept quiet not talking to people because at the state hospital there were unhinged patients that committed misacts of assault. Security monitoring was 24/7 on intense guard duty on high alert surveillance to mollify dangerous subjects. I had to be med-compliant, otherwise, I would be pinned down, shaken to the ground with Thorazine injected to make me sleep. I had to follow rules and regulations being less melodramatic so cooperation would quickly end the days sooner, that I'd be released transported back to in Naples. Plain and simple Philosophy foundation to believe. If you grow up and adapt in a constant abuse setting with 0 lack of credibility, of course there is going to be prevalent crime from violence in the dwelling atmosphere. Any hope for optimism was criticized. I knew I needed a vacation but the topic goes indistinct sunk below the bottom of the barrel empty respect and decency for appetite. Detailing back to my detention stay at the state hospital, I found the first few days uncomfortable. I got plenty of sleep during restless nights from a bed with a hardened mattress and the room was cold about 59 degree F o. I was freezing to kill germs. At nights I grew hungry where staff technicians only served 3 meals a day. They served nutritious meals from a protein, 2 sides of a carbohydrate, a fiber, a milk and a dessert. The hospital food was a better upgrade quality than what was served in jail for a stay sustained pertinent for only 5 months. During the day we had to attend a class for incompetency training. I was found ITP back at the jail, meaning incompetent to stand trial at the time to have my trial for the jury, the judge, and the witnesses to see the evidence in the discovery and inquire what took place to when the crime occurred. I felt like I was back in kindergarten learning my ABCs and 123s again. I was embarrassed and ashamed, but the process was mandatory to attend the meetings and classes, had I expected to leave the state hospital. There were subordinary classes that taught gardening and economic development, how to make useful investments. I benefited from the classes, but they seemed pointless that I would use the tools of information after I'm one day released out of custody. Good chance not, unless, I get a full-time job with benefits to start a portfolio for yearly investments for a Y2K or 301B options. I also attended religious services for Christian and Catholicism classes. I enjoyed being in the presence of God and the instructors that gave holy communion to refreshen my broken body necessary to rebuild my soul. It was an initial recharge for a good lead to a new beginning closer towards freedom. I kept my bed and room pristine, because administrators often checked our rooms to acquire inspections so there was no detected suspicion drug contraband of illegal paraphernalia smuggled into the dorms, even weapons. If we kept our rooms neat and clean we would be rewarded a pizza party. I earned 3 pizza parties before I was discharged from the state hospital. There would be days a movie would be played in the guest public speaking room to the residents. I didn't speak to none of the residence unless directed, not a soul, maybe one or two. Security permeated throughout the facility perimeter having to breakup the fights. I was assaulted confronting a bully. I had to attend a nurse's station for treatment for a swollen forehead. I didn't fight to protect myself, only because I didn't want to practically prolong my stay. So I kept my chin up encouraged that I was going to get out of it and my head covered that I wouldn't get injured. The more you engage in a conflict the longer your stay extends at the state hospital with limited expectation to leave on good terms. Some of the men at the hospital have either died or don't leave for 5 years maximum sentence, which equates a 5-year prison term sentence for a 3rd degree felony conviction. The situations grew uglier everyday towards dismissal. I had social workers, case managers, psychologists, and psychiatrists examine me their constituted facts determined about my case. The forensics evidently contributed a conclusion that I have Bi-Polar type 1 disorder with episodes of Schizophrenia-Effective Mania. I was declared openly that I have a behavior wellness defect. I was shocked that a coffin had been placed in my chest for my heart and a cage for my brain to be locked up; if you imagine. The forensic team denied justification for my testimony and found my statements inept of conflicts obtain home. They believed I was just plain delusional engineering a fraudulent story, experiencing an illusion from my subconsciousness. I showed the forensic team that a partial side of my face had been disfigured from the brutality I withstood in the abusive setting. They didn't see the apparent demarcation. *"Fascism,"* the team resisted to review the difference of symmetry in my face. I had no appropriate supporting defense on my side. I trusted no one. The mental hospital was an unnecessary punishment control of my captivity. It made my recovery unclear for a criminal hostage circumstance of an innocent normal man baker acted by the deceptive science of someone else's s coercion framed of me of deceit in a crisis. I was competent, but also compounded in the process to proceed. I was overwhelmed by the judicial process to cohabit with my public defender out of an inclusion of fear. I was misjudged and mishandled by the judicial process in Collier County. That's basically what the county and state does should you refuse to comply with your defense attorney. After being a week in a mental asylum, because that's what it was, I saw a judicial magistrate for a med-management assessment hearing. I was to be put on a medication, I've never been on before, for assessment as a daily regiment to cooperate full extend of conditions to hospital policy procedure; or should I refuse, I'd be administered an dosages of injection for . I reexplained clarification that I use natural herbs, foods, and exercises for behavior health improvements for my condition. My advice was initially infallible. My convinced convenience was erased consideration to be replaced with court orders and to take new anti-depressant medicines. I would be oblivious to the unaware constituent product what reaction distraction, going in the wrong direction digressed, would have a false positive impact on my body and how insecure the compound contingent affected my behavior against my liberties. I wasn't treated as an American patriot when sanctioned into custody, but a ticketed number among other patients being experimented by crime, control,and captivity against my Constitutional rights. Remember *"no mental reservation or purpose of invasion"* should also apply to the civilian besides the military cadet, because although civilian life aren't ranked soldiers, we are fighting wars against the psychotropic drug epidemic wars in league of the pharmaceutical drug dealing cartels liberal doctors since the 1960s. I was victimized in pursuit of my righteous identity. After 5 months of being in the mental hole of the state hospital debacle, I was discharged in handcuffs in a closed police unit vehicle. The truck was dark. There were no lights for me to see out guarded windows. I was locked in shackles. I didn't return to Collier County immediately, but Ft. Meyers where unusual, I stayed the night in a locked cell, stripped naked under suicide watch. I'm never suicidal, but patrol units were ordered to take extra precautionary countermeasures of any consequence against the prisoner. I had to wear a velcro vest. I looked like a turtle through the night. But by the time I returned back to my own county, I was allowed to change back into my own clothes. So after 5-long restless months I returned back to my jail cell in Naples. Things changed since I left the jail and someone inmates I knew left. I had 1 year credit time served which was pointless for me to testify at my trial. By the time I left the detention center, I would leave serving good terms recuperated my entire recovery development of condition with restored competence. I was released and discharged from jail October 2016 just a little under the date of the new year since the indicated arrested for the crime which positioned me into the slammer. I was placed to stay at the same homeless shelter before the 1st crime, registering for an open vacancy as a new resident and signing an authorized under health information privacy agreement. Familiar nostalgia resuscitated, since I originally was a resident Fall of 2010. A bedding, 2 sheets, a blanket and a pillow was provided for me including toiletries. My mom packed a blue tote carrier luggage bag with clothes, accessories and necessities for my stay, while I was sentenced by the courts to serve 3-years probation, early termination for good behavior, but 2, being 1-year was credit-time served in jail, and behavior health court for 1-year service attendance mandated with med-compliance. I analyzed each transformative scenario of control integrated while I went from one present depiction of confinement to another form of captivity transparent. I was mischaracterized a nomad nuisance, misconceived that I kept getting shuffled moveably, because of the horrendous monstrosity in a cultural changing decade. I was a 2-time typical repeated offender. Things had an impact affect absorbing its bold toll on me. At the shelter, I worked in the kitchen to serve hot meals to the poor residents. We made delicious dinners donated by benevolent people donated to the homeless community through staff provided philanthropic charity throughout the shelter to the needy. On Sundays we would have religious services by attending a church of our preference we desired to attend. The residents had to strip their beds every Tuesday to fumigate for insects and bed bugs to prevent illness contamination. Mondays were mandatory meetings and announcements. Rules of the facility were debriefed in the cafeteria, progress reports, and disciplinary pointers of practice had been taken into consideration should facility policy be broken. Birthday updates were announced by staff to tenants of those celebrating. Every Monday morning the facility transport services van would be available to drive individuals to their doctor's appointments, and clinician services were available coinciding the mental health clinic. I've been solidified Psychiatric-Statism for a decade. Employment purposes for searched employment opportunities previously referenced, I would attend the career resource center which was a program recruiter for resume' building skills, in addition cover letter development to put in applications for job placement. From the 8:00 AM to 2:00 PM shift in the afternoon residents weren't allowed to be on the premisses by strict orders of the homeless center. So in our own free time people had to actively find gainful employment and sustain diligently busy during the day seeking useful work, or be working making paycheck to pay expenses as living arrangements grew increasing difficult for adapting inept survival. I kept my chin up high, knowing incredibly, I was going to get through this discombobulation compression of frustration conflict to confront. I often communicated with family in New Jersey for a support system instrumentation element of encouragement, regaining an engine of confidence to avoid isolation in a state of misery. I shielded myself of uncertainty outcome around me, and in front of me in the community with excerpts from the bible. I was pleasant to the residents and was sincere, as I went through this repeating stage again in my life to resolve. I had to reeducate myself disciplined on a platform of discipleship for sufficient self-control, not letting go an instability of inner-peace for an outer balance. I was beginning to learn why I went through the impact of this worse case scenario, that happens to lots of people on a daily basis. This quest was a 2nd experience meaningful for learning a valuable lesson to let go of pride and earn reliable humility to serve the masses of the unfortunate population to amend reconciliation. It's an expectation of greater conscience. ***"Be a smart player instead of being outsmarted a cheater or a gambler of risks. Know the risks involved and stay away from the fire, but rather put the fire out. Don't be an adolescent and play with the fire. Be mature*** *to extinguish the fire with the proper chemical it's vulnerable to dissipate. Don't get caught up in the wrong crowd and walk the straight path not the wrong road. Don't live a crooked life which will lead to prosecution of the system and persecution of judged condemnation from others who don't have any bright intelligence of what position you're in. Keep forward staying neutral having favorable optimism of the outcome,"* the holy spirit of the Lord was saying to me. On December 17th, 2016 I published my 2nd best seller book, incredible to be noted to my book resume' record of career path. My beginning advantage of authorship writing achievement was 2-books closer to resonate in the world, out of the sand and baptized in the water for people that want a expressionism of redemption. After that phase of my life ended, that would the final conclusion, I sword, I would conform to revolutionized restitution to no misbehave against the system again. So I did and gave it all to Christ. I didn't rely on my own understanding, but applied assured reliance on my own patience and through humility and little effort of virtue I was brave enough to go home never going back to the state hospital. I contemplated on this message that would be the foundation for propensity escapade necessary for advantage to strengthen back to society. *"For there is no other name under heaven, give among men, but which we can't be saved." ~Acts 4:12.* It's comes to terms and conditions of calling the name of Christ when in treacherous territory succumbed that in instance of potential recollection vital to evoke the name of Christ in support to rescuing out of your dilemma, then resting on the will of God to perform the emphatic rest of the miracle to erase your crime; it loosens your control and free you from captivity. In support to that reference, that excerpt automatically assumes indirectly postulated that Christ is the only supreme being of heavens, earth and the universal dimension between. The intellect of apparent knowledge to understand overstates there are no other gods or beings that are supreme being to replace or filling Christ's shoes as Lord so he's maker and creator of life absolute for those that want to be exonerated of crime, saved from control and fled the confrontation of captivity. Christ the redeemer is the ultimate solution of judgment.

CHAPTER 6

HOUSEHOLD CONTROL

Moving into the new Naples condominium was a stressful process from NJ. We didn't take the time to adapt the natural surroundings around the neighborhood of the interior design that took months to develop. We had abusive neighbors and a landlord often disturbed, confronted us as offensive of the smallest shenanigans than the opposite ruptured scenario after scenario of derogatory compulsive harassment. The psychology process to function with rivalry truce was weak to reconcile. When complicit misacts of my horrendous arrests happened, our thoughts of moving down to the subtropics of a counterfeit paradise was a fantasy unimagined. It wasn't kosher, but a catastrophe. Instances of resentment experienced by myself, impacted me. I got the impression I was being excluded out of the condo. But my heart was unable to stay because urges of vibrations for momentum to return to the acting scene kept visiting my memory, reminding me visible I wanted to return and regrow my career that I once knew I would never accomplish.

However, I knew my present fact of truth was unpleasant because I relocated away from my friends, had to reset my working condition affairs to restart looking for employment, and the agony adamant wanting to go back to NJ where my heritage originated was going to change bringing a challenge, because being in a different environment was waking up to maturity. The act of sagacious responsibility acknowledged was settling in my subtle mind that people move out of their habitat state. Things change. You can't reconcile to the future once the past disappears the irreconcilable times dwindled. My relatives disburse to pursue their own career paths and you find your upbringing vanishes like the wind yesterday. I wanted to attend college for my Bachelor's degree at a post secondary school that never foisted a dream into existence, which I would need tuition. I was controlled in the dwelling as an adult by immoral tight authority of parental guidance, but also in captivity with community control competing at a level of state authority when history of complicit offenses repeated series of isolated incidences, only accidents overlooked. Being in confinement against psychological warfare with opponents, I could equate what POWS went through the torture camps in Vietnam or WWII emulated. It wasn't like that model. The circumstance were ugly. The fire was burning out of control unpleasant. The incident of my first crime injured a victim and I showed sympathy. Holding strong today, I and my rivals reconciled. We forgave and in forgiveness we removed 2020. But in FL previously there had been a caveat of precedented limitations and specific conditions as far beyond I would refuse to go. I was being treated as a petulant child for a grown man. The ages fluctuated downward as I grew older the maltreatment of maturity ratio, that was expressed rampant incognizant thinking in a hardheaded---dwelling. Age differentiation was a factor to the way I would behave to fit-in to the grownups, but even if I equated the world of others, being my own original person, I would get the scrutiny from others' opinions to explore my conscience of critical examination. Sedation by neutralization of the problem by administering a psychotropic agent seemed the only solution present which was the only apparent critical option represented and my liberty of my own decision was insecurity alienated. I told a member of my family up in NJ I had no where to go and required to escape the monotonous monstrosity of abuse. The mischief generated as a child is redeemable, but not remarkable as an adult, because people were hurt from the insolent privileges I cheated, that I injured emotionally. But by concept I had 1 relationship and it never evolved. My relationship flower never blossomed because I was a boat still in the harbor being alienated at home. After my 2 crimes happened, had they not manifested, I could of advanced to something in government getting a career position opportunity. But once you work in the Federal bureau, you lose precious competency in respect of your self-image and drudged accountability of righteous character. Your former self-identity disappears. The 2 crimes transpired was a wakeup alarm; it opened my eyes wider, sharpened my mind smarter, shocked my voice louder and cleaned my words transparent. I will never work in government. I don't want to be a drone to the slave of uncivil discourse. Once you take an oath of public office in 1 of the 3 branches of government you're some controlling administrator dressed in a nice suit and tie that would be contracted to subjacent officials to inject authority into another innocent knee-jerking amateur adolescent stupefied of his outcome that foreshadows the same position you were in once before you advanced than him. The irony is the patient is subjected to institutional captivity coping control evaluated, while the federal contractors in wolves' fur are ordering more control on the public decency and pumping criminal conspiracy to poison civilian victims against their rights of federal complicity. You end the patent of psychotropic pharmaceutical drug war epidemic for crime, control, captivity on the rival-group dwelling discovering cures, the epidemic density of dwelling domestic violence crime rate in the U.S. plummets freezing into to a safer comfort zone. The pharmaceutical drug epidemic wars stagger. Being in a rambunctious dwelling, I felt empty space in my head. I was filled with another's fuse instigated, pestered and mentally bullied through silence. I was frightened to communicate and practice speaking my Constitutional rights. Instances of my behavior were often constantly questioned with 3 haunting words and they were ***"what's the matter?"*** My attitude was confident, but misjudged subservient to concerned authority. That's when I analyzed psychological warfare was surrounding me around as the chess piece, straight to jail on the a game board, to either pay the debt or reap the consequence by going to jail for making your own ascertained assertion forming your own unsaid thoughts to find facts heard, what was transforming apparent into a real life experience. I'm the quiet character because staying quiet and doing as told by your parents, there won't be any inquisition to challenge fear and control for concern. Discouragement can be avoided by arranged intelligence and skill. But I stay neutral as often as I can, because that attitude demonstrates self-control and self-control is practically stereotyped what the world requires, that is underachieved virtue what we limit modern times legitimately. Frequently knowing a man's peace centered is often important to him. It discovers his reflection of identity, pursuit of better modified character, but however with noises in the dwelling the subject can disconnect a man's virtue, weaken his strength, and open wounds of deepened pain to remember a man's passed grief. I have a good relationship with my rivals. After my 2 criminal incidences, they gave me a 3rd chance after 2-baker acts and 2 criminal arrests most families would be immodest to disown their sons and daughters that go through that mischief rejecting forgiveness. They want what is best for me, to see that I myself must improve, recover, and reinvigorate my health. I told them that platform too. I also told them let me build important decisions by self-choice. Further acts of control and captivity will lead to additional violence and crimes that I want to stay clear of that atmosphere. One day, while on Christian radio, I heard a montage segment how abuse escalates in the dwelling. It's a premise to criminal activity by adolescents that become adults from behavioral changes of dwelling control and captivity. Yelling and outbursting pierces confusion in the mind that the shameful have no self-guilt into shouting performance of their actions. That's an example model of what I experienced at home for 10 years. I had sleep paralysis insomnia for 10 years from reminiscent memories of my crimes. I would be up for 8-10 hours for the duration throughout the entire night going into day. I got little shuteye. In the morning I would be awoken with loud talking of statements of communication happening between family conversations. I had no comfort. Should I notify the mental clinic, my medicines would be adjusted, or, replaced as treatment for displaced sleep misconstrued, rather than the irony, I be evaluated from the wearisome control in the dwelling. The 2 criminal batteries didn't ease the burden of being thrown out of the dwelling twice, but mentally magnified the haunted pain exposed impossible to hide. I had no-where to turn, no where to go, and no one I could trust except a couple of friends out of state who listened kindly to my case with care to my side of the story, until I was ready to reconcile with terms of myself and my family. Displacement in the core of my family's values and unity discombobulation exhibited alienated an internal affairs component of contract material integrated. I was treated as a stranger than a relative. I know I had to conform to socialized readjustment engineered. My readiness wasn't prepared to come home from the aftermath of the 2nd battery. I was getting use to being on my own, settling in on being self-dependent as an independent, than a compulsive co-dependent. I believed my mom used her discretion to forgive me. She did, and it took time a few years to reconcile towards adjustment. I knew she discretely forgave me, when then, I was allowed to have my own 1st apartment right down the street. It was a step-up studio apartment upgrade than being in dwelling control, from demand being captive as ordered around like a petulant child. But when I was in the state hospital I was angry with madness. I wasn't well-experienced in an unfamiliar way knowing psychiatric administrators could force me adjustments to transform my character. I'd be a different person, but I'd remember the anguish. This was my distress I was reliving, if admitted the adamant events happened in court. I forgave and forgot, moved forward and confidently conformed to God's standards above for using the practical methods of wisdom and philosophy of self-control power. Should I have testified after I left the state hospital, but didn't for credit time served and the charges dropped, I would have been found guilty and served 5 years in prison for attacking and innocent victim with a battery. I gave all the distraction back to the Lord. I believed in myself that God wanted to pacify that circumstance. ***"Don't seek revenge, revenge is mine but seek my refuge in me for I am victorious."*** When I was distressed with confusion, until I went to church groups and meetings I didn't go to their service conferences unjustified to hear a or conformed message that was delivered, but to identify with people that have been through the similar position frustration as I encountered. We would talk about stressful matters, read scripture, tell stories of passages from biblical accounts of scriptures taken place and integrate prayer. I just wanted to get away from the dwelling control, and the criminal penitentiary scenarios of parental prosecution from being stricken the captivity of needy institutionalism. I was still forced behavior health observation by medical experts in the system to receive continual treatment, as others admitted I exhibited awkward characteristics, so the impact of passed atrocities would not repeat in the future. I imagined, I was being a prisoner to psychotropic inquisition, and that which behavior health administrators used reports of childhood accounts connected to my adulthood behavior of history of offenses was justify I be monitored. My profound living arrangements in contrast to medical circumstances was like a product of commercialized paranoia, being sold by force not being bought by unrepentant witnesses around me; especially, from the lunacy in the matter of my mannerisms. When I was in the baker acts we had vitals taken immediately in the morning after we woke-up. I confessed I was a victim taking the psychotropic medicine to be compliant. The medical clinic presumed, because of intolerant behavior and patterns of unusual conduct supervised I was experiencing withdrawal. The technicians' concerns believed I was disruptive coping decompensation with a dysfunctional mechanism. Often in particular situations, my critics would have to confess in my behalf to an administrator of a facility to facilitate a performed procedure mistaken, that I had a dysfunction inability of poor limited competency to communicate the initial conditions of a random situation in order to reverse a task performed. I unsuspected legit concern what was happening when I could analyze my surroundings consistent. I would be left ashamed, because I wasn't allowed to explain my own predicaments, slipping into a hole attempting effort to climb out of a problem. I wanted to take charge of tasks with maturity and integrity undertaken without being burdened captivity. I was babied-bribes-negligent the valid compromise argument obligation sufficed self-confidence and self-control to govern my own destiny of life because of others' fears. That's changed through-thorough reeducation and patient instrumentalism. My critics assumed I was literally disabled by disinformation from the institutions and misgiven case as a lie. I had been misjudged arbitration to be controlled my whole life since birth by a slander conception of subversion framed in my position. This subject underscores a concept doses of Fascism were behind the aftermath of Socialism, which ordered an oligarchy on me by captive certain comprehensive restrictions. For the smallest things, I would be ridiculed outburst ridicule the biggest ordeals while explaining things in a simplified fashion. Talking would be internalized as yelling and expression would be mistaken for anger or viciousness by me when its wasn't. I was often vilified. Being diagnosed with Schizophrenia in the disclosure psychiatrists claimed, I must of inherited it genetically. Rare difficulty has a way indifferently to filter frustration disintegrated that is complicated mature, in handling a way of approaching a subject that carries resentment about that subject the refuse to object. To be blunt insecurities would carry incorrectly for about months putting strain on rival pressure and it incorporated hurt which I didn't deserve. The matter dissolved and I pacified its disorder. So perhaps should I have a disability uncontrolled in denial or a dysfunction of ***"behavior wellness"*** it was through the bizarre awkward experience being pressured a petulance in the presence of mishandling my erratic emotions always spinning in an incessant tangent. There was no rationality when I would negotiate a truce in an argument or peace aforementioned to dissipate a complaint. In the dwelling psychotic behavior tightened further uncontrollable restraint, as I mitigated solution to pacify distraction and intrusion distention away from offering assistance for performing a friendly gesture to my critics in courtesy; like, getting her a glass of water or getting someone something to eat being camaraderie. I would be asked to sit straight in my chairs at the dinner table when eating, policed how to respond to proper dining manners. This was of paranoia.

That wasn't the prevalent case. I didn't intervene in opponent's arguments to settle them calmer, because I didn't judge whether I was going to incorporate more fuel to the disagreement or someone might get assaulted by a crime of a domestic violence scenario. I was cautious of the consequences. As I slept throughout the night there were sounds that couldn't keep silent pacified in patients. Their demeanor was loud and boisterous. I wanted to sleep early night to late morning to get enough 8-hour sleep to build my energy. I'm not a early person; unless, I'm working an AM job which requires my presence early AM to report to work or a doctor's appointment. My sleep was disrupted. I was further fatigued on a frequent basis. The foundation of my euphoria was immobile. I could't operate effectively without getting a silent night's rest endless of bombardment noises undeserved. In the past 21 years from 1999-2020 my opponents surrounded me with condescending attacks alienated defenseless from protection. I scoped by assessment, after I mellowed out the last year of the 2010s. There was the demonization crime of ridicule, the harassment memories, the bellicose of attacks, the nonstop endless rampages arguments of hostility and animosity confronted. So what I experienced was emotional violence between parties before my 2 crimes and the aftermath lunacy coped from between rivalry digressed excessively. I nonetheless sometimes lectured my opposites encouragement with confidence and self-esteem, but they only envied themselves a paralysis of discouragement and coma of disappointment. I cheered to reinvigorate them some faith. But you can't force to change people a crumb of authentic transformation. I've independently been praying for their health and common sense, but all I got were episodes of ill-legit derision. So like an atoll or island sinking into the sea, my atoll or island was sinking into the sea absent of the blueprint to glue the ship together staying afloat, that being my heart, and I quite couldn't put all the rhetorical pieces amended back reintegrated. I stayed out of certain places of the dwelling to get away from the outbursts. The instant scenario really brought anxiety and crashes of depression. The pain was like a conscious aching burden of affect anchoring anxiety sunk anguish on my soul, pounding and thumping nervousness on my chest. I had the hardest job in the world psychologically. In the meantime, I missed opportunities on the liberties of my independent agenda I knew abnormal changed things becoming different at random indifferent times I was in a loophole crisis. I went to Jr. college, but I never had the experience, the social impact, and friendly-fun gathering of friends getting together to hangout more often social gatherings that we together would all one day be guests to an indispensable wedding that would be one day be my own. I wanted to know what that celebration felt-like in a group to enjoy the enthusiasm of getting married, falling in love to fulfill a sacred bonds of matrimony, having a courtship, and a full-time paying career. I'm the legit responsible subject actively controlled on psychotropic chemical compound agents for therapeutic lies. The discretion of liberal slander disburse liability, that I have stagnant mental challenges of rubbish, than, to persevere going the extra distance to start my own family the same rights as other privileged Americans. There is a red flag I admit with my personal health disposition that projects a disorder, I have think harder and have imbalance of my thoughts before I speak skipping my words in my voice which is a common disorder challenge indicator about my ability to perform my character. So perhaps the the health administrators have an edge of advantage revelation of showing accuracy research they examined professionally. My generation is already passed its prime and most 1/10 of 99.9% of women I encountered now my age, or a bit younger have children, already married inside or outside the gargantuan service of wedlock. Sure I can do an electronic dating profile insignia match on a dating website for fun, but how many profile's aren't web scammers for your wallet or bank account to steal from you? I play it cool and safe. I disconnect an elusive fantasy distant from the crime-spree adversity of scam captivity. My opponents had a habit of misleading instructions explained in a particular design that is frustrating to understand inconsistent to follow. I would be bathed reverently of illusive imagination by mental and strenuous tyranny. I would communicate a notion of ideas or dictate different element entities of information to do something empathetic, opposite rivalry would objectify ex-communication of senile hatred responses in pugnacious anger, condescending remarks, and a capacity of detrimental innuendos in the disestablishment line of peace unloaded injury I received from rivalry. As the generation began to replace my generation, I was beginning to get the impression of attention I always anticipated sought I would slow down. My circumvented needs were exiled. The restrained control in the dwelling was the devil in the details included a circumstance dilemma that discombobulated my opponents for days and weeks spinning uncontrollable. I would be subjected an aversion, joining the misery index of being implicated pertinent situations affecting a cultural world

twirling anyone's apocalyptic mind. I encouraged---
enthusiasm for relations to resolve, not the dilemma-drama
of mania to evolve and revolve. The foundation of the
dwelling back in FL has been an experimental barrier being
with other sloppy recovering addicts, where I never engaged
in contraband paraphernalia. The trapped-situation marked
me as an experimental guinea pig, a fish caught, and a
suspect under endless arrests integrated in a surreal setting
of captive control anarchy. I suffered repercussions, surveilled
institutionalism by clinicians they were: policing what I do,
where I go, what I say, how I act, my character performance
in the community by policy of the behavior health clinic's
immediate practices I had coped. This was Liberalism in
operation. Opponents plan of observation was intended
viable for my vivid accountability of accidental criminal
history of offenses to hold me in detention indefinitely.
Mandated orders were a required synthetic recovery plan to
be watched always by practitioners' demand of the clinical
behavior health community under tight evaluation. All hope
of returning to a normal priority life repudiated to be a free
man again, as I always been persecuted for 2-isolated
incidences vanished; instead, of suppressed criminal history
that had been documented in reviewed public record an an
insult to injury. I was inspected-consistent in the correction's
system discussed confidential by teams of medical officials.
Living in Naples didn't escalate my case restored. To
exaggerate, after losing the popularity demand of my 1st
superhero novel invention and my dramatic objectivity of
my philosophy tool book earning a 9.68 national book
review of almost a best seller's book on the list, I felt declined,
but imprisoned banished reward as distraction away

regaining any confidence of retained fame. I disbelieved I had a shot at worthy attention to become further popular due to lack of resources, representation, and management. I became estranged to the fear of resentment for having a normal non-surveilled legit incognito life. Should I gamble the big time in showbiz, I'd have to pay loopholes in taxes required, be caught in the tirade of politics, and limit the quality relationship of making friends, even sustaining recent friends. Gain of showbiz and fortune comes brining repercussions of the apathetic territory for infamous consequences. It would mean I would be a known featured icon figure exposed to the globe. After the 2 criminal incidences so blunt obfuscated which happened, not wanting to dwell on them, because emotion would have had a gravity on me, returning where I previously lived was unwelcoming more like a stranger and treated indifferent in an awkward unpleasant manner, than was before since the legal dramas transpired. I returned home in an elusive reality set in mind, that it was like a dream irreversible to awaken. Would there be pacifism in the atmosphere after my erroneous torture? The outbursting was indistinguishable as mental statism, taunting but intensified, while I objected it. Should I have procured the perimeters of Schizophrenia, the series of trauma I confronted throughout the years of social decline upheaval, that repeated itself in dwelling frenzies, irregularly unmaintained by my opponents that they refused practice to terminate? I stood my ground. Years of brutalization almost had me scarred hysteria. I remain functional, but not facilitated efficiently punctual at the competent general normal-rate level of the seldom mainstream population unless quarantined med-compliance on pharmaceutical compound derivative therapy. Where's the accountability in my evident perseverance of being equally independent? Can we still apply the epidemic content of Constitutionalism for a cure? In my valid opinion understatement disrespected by a wave of general rivalry. Yes we should. The real authenticity bluff is, I must be designed to be remade to accept others' falsified approval for consenting superior equality than me. It's an aversion of ultra intolerance. Conformity requires permission to practice intolerable authority refusing rejection; instead, of prosperity to the best of my ability through my liberties forfeited by statist control objecting Nationalism.

CHAPTER 7

RECOVERY MEETINGS

From the initial point of getting out of lockup from jail the first time, I attended Christian based recovery meetings. The homeless shelter had some designated voluntary Evangelical-based meetings connected to the expanded foundation of biblical truth and study at 7:00 PM, 2-hours every night after dinner. On Thursdays we had a private conference with a teacher who is a famous mechanic auto-shop small business owner of car mechanic shops in Naples. It's his rediscovery in Jesus Christ that led him to teach bible study classes at our local town's homeless shelter. I listened to eulogies, did my do-diligence to follow the pointers, took notes, and followed stories that covered the unprecedented chapter of Matthew 20 when the accounts of biblical application evidently documented Jesus Christ taught 10 laws out of the 66 books of the bible on the Mount of Olives, when he gave the sermon on the mount. I remember vividly an important lesson that was a subject valuable, that was a vehicle foreshadowed the unjustified dilemma I was burdened with wholeheartedly. Jesus Christ said in Matthew 7:5 ***"Hypocrites remove the beam from you own eye then you'll see clearly enough. You must remove the specter or beam from your eye, than you'll see clearly enough before you remove the plank from your brother's eye."*** Meaning, first you must spot the source that's the cause of the problem rendering a conscious decision to help your fellow brother first, lifting or unloading his gravity before you can reverse that same catastrophic circumstance conflicting you. You must remaster control of the wheel steering you the right direction and not misdirected when disembarked off course. I honestly adapted that clarified passage brilliantly charged strength with a better grip embraced control, lesser, than the challenges. I practiced using this passage for sharpening my character. Like in Psalms 27:17 says ***"Iron Sharpens Iron and One Man Sharpens Another."*** I attended a men's breakfast recovery meeting for rebuilding lives and hope for fallen men in 2017 and 7 out of the 12 months of 2018. I remember a friend who was on the program's board of trustees assigned me a job to cook morning breakfast for the integrity of the gentlemen. The morning meeting was an exciting experience, because I was around people that modeled me rebuilding their lives, reconditioning the perimeters of dark areas affecting them they were battling and redeveloping the artistry demonstration of my creativity capacity, dramatically I could perform. After the meetings I stayed afterwards to attend my contribution to assist cleaning up the conference room. The programs were outstanding. We were talking about the inner-spirit of the God vs. the outer flesh of man, breaking down barriers of sin and righteousness because how Jesus Christ endeavored to fulfill the unconditional love of God's eternal spirit that rescued the impotent meek for the guilt of their salvation. We clustered and brainstormed table discussions scattered into group discussions. When I joined the morning breakfast group with the elder gentlemen, I fell into a position of transitory placement. My doubts and dismay understood thinking about the dwelling passed mistakes did vanish from memory with temporary replacement of keeping occupied. My precedented mixed feelings about the dilemmas that burdened me disappeared. But I wouldn't anticipate meeting friends or someone around my age, not even a woman for a casual relationship would at be worst of bay because of the factors assumed people of insecure opinion could check my background records, and would criticize me captive of those characteristics with malice. The 2010 crime was a hard process unforgotten. I survived the challenge. I conquered the initiation. The 2015 crime was an irreversible action, pain in the details, I regretted hardly the chains that tied me and weighted anchored down my mind held against me. The meetings allowed me to procure my coherence of grievances. I corresponded well participating in groups, contributing to random allegorical questions of practical terms of biblical application usage in needful circumstances, and applying elements of philosophy in important urgency of daily performances. After years of my dramatic impact of behaving as a nuisance seeking the holy spirit of God, rendered me under transfiguration of holy redemption. I then decided to write this book to collect the documented recorded details journeying on my quest healing in story format. Making stewardship of friends facilitated. I blended in the recovery meetings, which was easily indicative, the intent of building discipleship. That was the intent of integrating God's content in the system of contentment restored opposite of conflict. That inscription translated, I also interpreted, was to practice teamwork with others as an influencing prayer. The recovery meetings were a recourse in my treatment plan towards recovery; another spin of care towards balancing my cure escalated my competence. The meetings taught me not be envious of my neighbor and translate application of biblical character that would free me from the deranged imposition of my control and captivity I resented. I started reading a self-help book about the contrary difference of faithful and faithless emotions that personified encouragement to avoid: doubt, misdoubt, mistakes, failures, disappointment, discouragement, self-guilt, pride, envy, pity, sorrow, grief, misery, anxiety, and worry to focus my all my attention on the self-image of God. I started reading the book, feeling, I was making a connection with the holy spirit. I can sense the frequency with Christ. The skies were opening and a waterfall was pouring its spirit flowing my mind with the heavens. A vibration was corresponding to the light of the Lord. I read an excerpt from 1st Peter 4:19 that says ***"those that also suffer shall entrust their spirits to faithful creator in doing what is good."*** I meditated on that subtle meaning trying to making sense on that message. I judged wisely often. I prayed in session to hold a conventional conference with the Lord asking him "what is it He interpreting to me?" He was conveying a message to me saying: *"you have already pledged your allegiance prayed to me, you have given up your spirit to me, you have suffered and persevered in my name and worthy to be my child, for you are* *a greater good."* He entrusted wisdom instilled in me. I've been given a gift of intelligence, another chance of brightness containing brilliance from all my captivity benefited from God, not limited longer-burden that he was my auspicious gift. Going to explicable meetings frequently dwindled my doubts about my passed mistakes that reenforced the principle-pointers of the promising book I read. The message was registering emphasis that there are happy endings and beginnings coming to terms of endearment, for confronting an endless pugnacious battle of progressive tyranny. The consternation of libel chastisement from Neo-Marxism drama rippled during all the years of control of unacceptable captivity unsettled returning back home the whole time. I attended the an Episcopal church in Naples 2017 and 2018. It was a gentlemen's coalesced gathering social conference meeting every Wednesday at 6:25 PM. The mission requirement was to take disciples of Christ integrated with the passages from the word in the bible and transform brothers of Christ for each other changed as soldiers in the kingdom of God. We did introduction, 3-title songs intended for the evening, memory verse, then sermon by the lead senior supervision pastors. We exchanged few words then we were provided a program with individual questionnaires of the current approached application to the material title-topic subject we were covering that night. We broke into groups. I felt I was growing with pragmatic symbolism in the glory to the spirit of God answering the questions with suitable answers. I provided a reliable answer in an instant, but my legit opinion that I confessed from my statement from my table group didn't seem to endeavor any persevered option to respect the facts of my confession. They found my expression of my answers unintelligent, and misconstrued objective listening. That point momentarily is when I realized, I chose not to further attend the church because of the shady secular unusualness taking place in the congregation; it left me feeling the treatment was coldhearted, hardheaded, and egregious, stereotyping the unquestionable chilling pagan element in the fellowship system. I didn't fit in. I believed the dependency of having to go to a religious seminar, because my opponents recommended it, was a methodized practice to turn my darkest situations isolating me further than recovered. I internalized the impact of vicarious secular fundamentalism traditions taking place in the church. I kept getting the run-around of apostasy intercrossed in misdirections. Directors and visitors of churches facilitated me to attend X=Y and Y=X around the rosy in various churches shoved back and forth vicariously, twisting my mind with invalid untruth that limits valid transparency. I was enlarged disgust by rules of discomfort. I kept comfort of my relationship with my faith private, but disavowed the captivity of being confined to a church because of density indoctrination that is exercised world-wide. The meetings picked up all the pieces and the pieces firmly fit-in the puzzle to adjust my condition. The big picture of recovery fit once, but not frequently. In fact I benefited the rewards of joy, confidence, peace, patience and self-control (Galatians 5:22) at an Evangelical based church where the Thursday night's dinner and meetings were held than Saturday morning breakfast. Had I known better than my power of understanding before, fact is, my 2-legal dramas and 2-baker acts previously would have been prevented, had I grown wiser subsequent than now proficient.

My wisdom would have been more prevalent and been more of a useful tool sensibly to dictate my actions. I would have judged my emotions controlled invulnerable in correspondence to my relationship with God pertinent to resist me from the definition of community trouble.*"The fruit of the spirit is love, joy, peace, kindness, kindheartedness, gentleness, faithfulness, patience, and self-control."* (Galatians 5:22:) I made the bed of my curse, the enigma which is the mystery of wisdom to my dilemma-version to depicting the fruit of my spirit. I know my fruit was sour because of my behavior using that paradigm model to my former reprehensible character. That I needed to adapt knowledge and intellect for my fruit to become riper. My captivity of controlled mistreatment and progressive parental tyranny in the past was like a tree I planted. If you imagine. Now there were 2-deciding factors to the case of ripe or sour fruit, whether my plant would get enough water and sunlight to grow or decay, and then die unlearning principles of anything imperative. If the tree decomposes I'm still trapped in the circle of despair blaming myself overwhelmingly regrettable not detaching the past. Disgust would lead to confusion because having self-guilt not dissipating the criminal mistakes of blaming others that have devastated me caused pain. I then would know I'm defenseless having a disadvantage to seek justice except the subversion damage that has been done. But if my tree grows the fruit will be sweetened with new memories to make-up for loss of time with family and friends. I'd create a new memory file of records in my mind to replace the pain of collateral damage prior to major incidents reoccurred returning to FL, reemerging a recourse for strength. I would possess that special light of God under my feet, and my mind under his wings shielded for protection referring back to scripture. I can't go back to reconcile the broken window of wreckage that occurred, but by writing this book of recovery, memory, and redemption will ultimately reinstate my worst case position for future opportunities restored to blossom award, than did the passed case dispositions denied. Good rule of thumb you administer. You know how you regain value? You prove to others, performance of your actions broken down slowly for others to be convinced of your honesty, earns trust in small steps. Estimate that your competent ability can establish to heal earnest attitude of character among others. Avoid judged understatements as a rule for insults. I learned these essential pointers in Anger Management: ***"Say what you mean, mean what you say, don't say or do a mean."*** 2011-2013 I attended a Friday night dinner, praise, worship and workshop biblical class at my local church. It was free to attend. There was a game room you can play games, sing songs, worship, meet people, get acquainted familiar with other Christian-based people going to ministry classes subsequently to learn the application biblical facts with filtered scriptures to read, review, and translate God's entity accounts of written stories. It's no different than other meetings with different lineup of activities coordinated, but we all get the indistinguishable message paraphrased. The irony is the experience version of classes of getting correlated information, is retold in a revolutionized format from a dissimilar location. Students at the church took a test on the application studies of subjects for 3-5 weeks every Friday of 1-month covered material in an isolated particular book from the bible. I took the test and received a 100.0% score. It was an amazing memory that monumental-moment endeavoring to learn something new everyday so self-evident. Our first assignment assessed was to read the book of John, then reverse the reading order with Matthew, Mark and Luke disarranged in the New Testament 4 pillars of heaven. We discussed about how when our peace is disturbed, when someone loses our trust, when we get discouraged, how people rediscover their groundbreaking faith, how people are transfigured disciples are called the serve through elevated service, submission and sacrifice finding opportunity for in God brings satisfaction available for our self-worth contrary to contradiction. Different topics were covered, expressed, and the anecdote scoped subjects were researched in standard consideration. Then, I exercised these tools as vehicles corresponding my fiasco dilemma always in the parent trap of crimes, impacted control and pressured captivity orchestrated in among the intimidating drama of rival antipathy. I self-required a promise to collect and gather as much intelligence on the bible having an open relationship with God as much as I can, while, I was compromised on a rough sidewinding crooked-road among social displacement in Naples. I succeeded my relationship on track emancipating that relationship with Jesus Christ, handling the act of my condition with care. Before my first criminal incident occurred which was only an isolated accident, being open minded, I recommended to the family we all see group counseling to resolve pugnacity, not revile the situation further confused into purposeless vitriol. I recommended family counseling after my family and I moved back to Naples 2010. There was frustration with my behavior overseen. My conduct was misconstrued by analytical insecurity. I knew a group effort than one person seeking pacification would be beneficial to strengthening terms of serenity for the family. When I attended these Evangelical meetings the recommendation inquisition for therapy vanished, having no bearing idea to attend, being equipped with fortitude. The subject was no longer confined into circumvented impression to continue facilitation with any subtle reform program. The plot was shallow to dive--- escaping the storm of the story to return to a normal prognosis. The prognosis of a clean engine to escape the psychotropic insurgency and getting on a miracle script platform of Nationalism, a free and state mind dependent on expressionism, was impossible without the progressive invasion of clinical sciences. As we got to the nineteenth year of the 2010s close to entering the 2020s. I became med-compliant. I estimated and established a pacified code of conduct being on a suitable-substance to be well-acquainted on an agent that would stabilize my mode of ego, my rational thinking and aggression. No aggression rises should something or someone vilify my line of defense to defend my reputation dignity, because the fetal upset decline of testosterone chemistry is imbalanced. My voice doesn't explicably sound deeper like other men and still sounds like a teenager or a fruity adolescent kid. I won't seem to grasp rejection of a technicality through the robust refusal of criticism from individual adversaries non-acquainted in our culture, because of the chemical implantation of new mandatory psychotropic modern-day biochemical sciences. This is only my opinion, my ascertainable assertion, but I believe the anger management class is a surrogate class that adds more injury than cure because they teach you techniques to avoid anger, not to grow a backbone to confront your attacker bullies in the worse case scenario positioned from attacks. Chemical components of certain medicines silences the sword of your soul trembled still, than, to resurrect that soul of strength necessary appeared to expel your rivals. The anger inside of you where you get your testosterone or liquid strength HGH natural chemical growth hormone in your body you need to create a standoff and prevent criminals from attacking you is insulated. Today it's reverse. You can't expel it because, how, from a legal standpoint the compression of criminal authority is so restricted knowingly and willingly what you say and do will charge you under arrest by law for protecting your life through self-defense methods. The West was won, but today the West is conceded that truce to be lost from the East and the South disconnected from the North through the outskirt territoriality mental-probing of patient condemnation. Before the meetings when I was a part-time public servant employee working a regular job, I was self-conflicted control of my own captivity. Come to think about its entirety, the subversive counteracted tyranny and abuse, with the forced psychotropic medication trip-up prescription agents that transformed me inefficient. It affected my corporate assembly line of work. In my past, I was violent and said statements behaved in a way that were atypically unusual that was unorthodox to the perception of unwelcoming compliments. I didn't measure up to the policy of favored agreement with relationship to store management. I got fired from the grocery store in Naples I worked at with mandatory referendum to stay away from the store; or, I would be arrested in police custody for trespassing. I read a chapter in the bible quoted in the New Testament that Christ finds favor in you and shows kindness towards one granting favor, as you show compassion shared with others. Well here I am writing another book to tell my story, my overwhelming circumstances overcame, and just continue to carry my cross for him, what and which objection of regret, approaches my way. Being in therapy helped, because it made up forgiveness for the misplaced years, the missing years of inefficiency which painted a scenario for all the guilty injury I had to restore and correct. I accept in my late to early to late 20s, that I admit, I was a naive. But as soon as I grew older, I didn't get the full-commissioned function of common sense projected, until had to read self-discipline books inclined for escalating my ability of competence to the next-level engagement through predictable understanding. My diligence of gravitating toward adapting knowledge of measurable wisdom for nothing, but immaculate purified wisdom to be adjusted suitable for the general public to downplay the cat and mouse tape of stereotyping judgment, was an independent requirement alone. The next phase to connect with Christ and have a relationship through him self-confidently imagined, was to read and notate as much words of his message to receive his spirit, and messages ministered of his voiced law. I wanted to keep confined precise in mind his burning optimism as much as possible. A fire devoting patience to make a righteous decision had conceptual time building. Advanced circumspection of advised council, with passages, interpreted practical application. Should I vividly think-back the introspection and remember the retrospected wounds of haunted events as a nuisance conducted, the facade walls are all going to fall down and crush me, because my mind was not in the direction of God's unfailing light, as they should be by keeping my eyes on his face and heart in his present salvation. I've already been forgiven by his blood shed of the sinful world. I have been sanctified by fixating my ears toward the words that are subtle in listening the message for the protocol programming to enable transformation, for those that yield transfiguration to be cleaned and flipped right-side-up erasing the sticking dirt of history. So to-do this sequence of transfiguration, I had to have a foundation of quiet-time to myself attending meetings of book materials, taking notes, reading, and executing balance. Sometimes I negated biblical conferences in transitory manner. But my scars and soars swelled permanent. The persistent-ramification concussions wouldn't fade, but revisited archives of my memory. Though-through-thorough denial that I was normal, the scars and wounds of mental paralysis was permanent. Adding chemical pharmaceuticals fluctuated the strength of the damage. The derangement of torture throughout the years of getting yelled at in a form of verbal senseless abusive tyranny to surface has exhausted me, and fatigued me as I repeated prior. I'm more disabled now than I was in the 2000s. I will imply the explanation of referenced details conveyed. There's also a random imprecise-presence of uncontrollable Schizophrenia I've been diagnosed. A component that held me captive feeling helplessly impotent occasionally incapacitated. I had experienced hell journeyed and returned nothing unimaginable of unquestionable suspense, than the worst hell ever visited brutalized for that 36 years. I carried my cross like Jesus Christ, emotionally hung from it. That intent by drama domesticated and controlled in not just the dwelling, but the community, has made the outlook appear grim to other people, that I'm not self-reliable to take care of myself, think for myself, survive and self-suffice my needs for resources persuadable from the subversion committed on me by notorious misappropriation of subversive torture. Radicalized tyranny inexcusably directed me to my wicked violent behavior in the past. It was the result of my criminal arrests, my backer acts and my explicable personality shown as a infamous scapegoat before I healed. The predicament then was the chemical imbalance invading its untimely scenario to appear, the deficiency of interconnected limited thinking, impaired judgment from Bi-Polar 1 Mania and Schizophrenia. The disorder disabled my work to focus ability from concern, causing that which these disturbances in the community lead other people to witness my troubles transpiring, mischaracterized me of the isolated source of my misbehavior. In the serious community I lived, I was not treated as person only labeled a patient from opinions. But what about the cure? That's excessive progressive Liberalism controlling the Conservative that is told never to grow up, get out, to become mature, to get married, and have children of their own. I always acknowledge the courteous respect provided, given from my family, and when I needed to take my medicine, even before as a functioning normal man. I said on a basis, if a foundation of cure is found, I wouldn't have to, as ordered, be forced to take any compounds. How Fascism has forced the younger generations indoctrinated fundamental to comply conforming to their cultural is substandard. That's an example why most people find the church dishonest and discover what they preach nullifies misleading. I fortunately didn't practice studying willful material or analyze the common sense consideration idea the beltway South; its tight restraint authority to empower you coping-control medication placement and attend meetings thinking that's always going to solve the case to the problem preloading the patient with psychotropic medicines, subjecting a man neutered or woman spayed neurologically as a domestic animal manipulating their consciousness. If the pharmaceutical companies knows diligently there are side-effects in these compound psychotropic agent derivatives, then dictated competence cogent, they would also realize they would reliably would counteract response to remove the prevented side-effects in compound derivatives on the markets, to fight the reaction exposed of the side-effects, making a marketing strategy illness circumscribed overlong periods of time against the consumer. I felt so blunt embarrassed that my intelligence was being overworked impatiently, being forced to act too stupid furthermore mind-melded by the shadow elite behind the Marxist iron curtain divided by a concrete wall. I felt my experience was rejected to mold my manhood escaped confinement. I hardly dated and rarely dated. I just had 1 unachieved relationship in college that lasted a few weeks to a month. have I had a suitable partner, a steady permanent girlfriend, I would be much more, rather than ironically credential, be of a transfigured man of incredible unity, distrusting unverified dating experiences on social media platforms from online interactivity. Should I have proprietary liberty to self-govern my own destiny in a nation of opportunity, inconsideration, I would't be controlled captive, mishandled a social community experiment assessed observed discretion from periodic clinical visits. A social relationship is imperative in a recovery plan to restore character, to creating a special bond of loyalty for prosperous marriage. A sabotaged condition is an awful position being isolated under dictatorship control. When rivalry implies authority the community mandate orders by clinical study mistakes of accidental criminal history, leaving behind a digital scar to prohibit forgiveness. The system of unforgiven criticism from duress of past chastisement is called ***"The haunted hostility syndrome."*** It's a situation of permanent practice when people in society will revile a victim's incidents of mistakes of the past. People will behave condescending towards victims' circumstances to project confusion. Blamed faults forced in invalid arguments will aggress hostility out of control to conform one insecure in self-guilt. Hostility of constraint control to conform one insecure of self-guilt is assessed. The conclusion will prevent someone to move clear ahead forward. Hostility of insecure control will conform them insecure as an individual experiences self-guilt from others' aggression. The conclusion will prevent the injured to clear emotion of action with motion to move forward in their destination.

CHAPTER 8

HIGH SCHOOL FLASHBACKS

Back in September 1998 I started high school in Naples FL. I remember reminiscent the flashback so vividly conspicuous. I had just road my bike next door from the apartment complex around the corner of the path to the roadway lane that would take me all the way a 1/4 mile to the school facility. This would be my start as a freshman, but would begin the days when the sun would rise in the horizon against me from others' bulling career of formidable rivals. The criminal gangsterism was prevalent from freshman years to the junior years but propitiated my senior years of slandering, the innuendos, the resentment and the chastisement against my name. As soon as I went to the high school new student orientation begin where to report, students were assigned class schedules and told to report in our homeroom with our teacher. Classmates were introduced for the first time that would be for 4-years of high school news, where we performed the pledge of allegiance, activities, student body council, faculty, teacher announcements, high school sport's statistics, after school programs and other amateur acknowledged important events that materialized and caught students' attention. In high school we always showed pride toward our home sport's team, as I showed humility towards earning outstanding grades. I was often shy, timid making friends, stayed recluse towards sitting with the jocks and talking to people. I ate my lunch with the students that were only in the specialized classes. But I felt embarrassed, because I wanted to be with the typical kind of mainstream students that were chosen to taken the FCAT, HSCT, and SATS that granted straight A's, high-ranking students, and a scholarship to a major university would be any fascination of toward a student's awarded dream, when he or she graduated high school. I never surpassed the level of valedictorian for high-ranking academic achievement, even earning 2nd best rewarded salutatorian, but with hard work I wanted, because I was disbarred from taking any random version of a high school competency test that would advance my position to a major state university of my decision, when I failed ineligible to contained the capacity of skills to do them, but untested. So decisions assessed data of the guidance counselors that misdirected and misinformed bias about my condition of IEPs to my parents, that the best education I can ever achieve is a vocational college, when I graduated high school. I disproved my critics' opinions and went to a community college in Paramus, NJ to have some form of a degree, an A.A. in Computer Science. I have a Jr. degree, just not a secondary school degree supplemental should I choose to further continue my course of education, enhancing the support instance of the case. I remember so congruently the days of my high school journeys, very so conclusively. I couldn't study staying awake to focus on my work material ritual largely enough, because I was enticed on 1st psychotropic medicine reactant dominant as a kid. I was discombobulated in confusion. Other students conspicuously misconstrued my character. I was misjudge to appear apparently ill when I wasn't. I was incognizant due to to my private health examination being treated for detriment pharmaceutical chemical therapy demanded by the pediatricians, insisted through my parents' request. The exhaustion and fatigue of the first 2-years of high school extracted the wind from my face and breath from my lungs. In my sophomore year, I was in gym class and fooling around anxious with a brut kid, older and stronger than me. He was wrestling against me. My left arm broke. I was in excruciating pain. First responder paramedics had to be called into the school gymnasium. They lifted me up on a stretcher with a temporary cast and plastic flap wrapped around my arm, until I got to the hospital for treatment. My arm was broken for 90 days until the crack in the bone hardened. I received an epidural for the pain. I was proscribed morphine so I wouldn't have constant pain 18-20 weeks for the healing process. That scenario event that took place in my life, when I was near 15 or 16, was the only depicted time my mom expelled any type of addictive drug that would recessively control me as a narcotic refused by the doctors. I avoided the morphine and sustained surviving the pain for the weeks' end. The kid that broke my left arm technically didn't understand what he had done. It was typically horseplay, but if I knew his character profile composited, I would have purported my story to the principal to suspend him for the damages done. I was subjected to my first personal injury from the pernicious criminality bullying among from a series of serious technicalities which transpired. There were other rivals and bullies before the glamorizing popularity expansion of social media platform technology really started to boom after the 2000s. One time in my junior to transitioning senior year, during a time during lunch, while I walked to retrieve my food someone slipped a paraphernalia drug into my chocolate milk. I fell asleep not digressing the details of the story until after I woke up. The chemical contents impacted me. I slept for minimum 4-5 hours home at the most at least until 8 PM. I remember captivity of my own conscience trying to remember, what my initial intellect competence recorded to the ability of my memory, and what had been assaulted by a vulgar narcotic perpetrated by my attacker. All I had was a theory because I didn't have material evidence of someone else actually witnessing another individual slipping a chemical derivative into my food contents to harm me. But I know I was drugged because my condition was performing differently, reacting awkward, coping inability to function usual. There was an underwhelmed crime subtly disburse happening within the facade of the school. I never filed a report addressing a complaint. I was naive on behalf of my own character. That person would have been interrogated and would have received either ISS or OSS suspension for the nature of the trouble inducing another student under the influence of indiscrete drug paraphernalia. I wasn't myself until at least 4-weeks later then restored. A case wan't investigated. I was at a frequent time framed crimes by fundamental behaviors of my rival bullies in my English or

Math classes that once put me in OSS suspension for 2 weeks. I wasn't allowed to go to my regular classes, but due to my issue I had to report to a small portable building 50 yards from the main campus. I was subjected a packet of saved schoolwork from all my classes to keep me busy for the next 2 weeks in a portable building. Should selective memory self-serve correction to me, I was involved in a fight with a bully gargantuan than I was. I was puny and petite. Either my sophomore year or junior year, I was weight training to get stronger, but this kid was a bull, massive, and a giant, but even though I was the one that was accused for defending myself, I conquered my attacker and overcame my giant from his Fascist behavior. I was the victim condemned contempt at fault. The tradition of bullying exists, so long as, Liberalism and Fascism exists, until the conflict is confronted and resolved the aftermath to repair one's reputable character. I had 2-weeks of makeup work meeting a deadline to finish and be caught up with my classmates in school. I was a product of shame going to school, then home. I remember as if I was cornered by the distraction of the bullying drama. A lot of the crucial attacks on my enemies were effective and I overcame them. At another point in my senior years, I took a on the job training class for school credits towards graduation. We would be assigned to report to a local job site transported by bus to volunteer collecting experience towards career development skills, students would incorporate usefully once performed in the work-force after school years. The characteristics I displayed were performing poorly on the job and resisting to pay attention of directions of my actions. Perhaps, it wasn't addressed sooner which should have been brought to light of the issue on the table further. The mental exhaustion which the bulling abuse fostered on me impacted drastically. Further damage applied to condition of my character compacted corrosion in myself from others, as I got older. I forced too much unconditional rampant misbehavior on innocent people, unquestionably aggressive, that didn't deserve to be compromised any discrepancy from me. My forgiveness to heal throughout the years was indescribable. I sought the services I needed to stabilize psychological balance, but insisted to medical practitioners to resist perpetuating institutionalism to be medicated. It was my intertwined relationship spent restless with God what restored my inward-soul to invigorate my outward-body. Now I notated patience realizing all too well, what I was induced as a kid growing inside, wore and tore me ripped slowly, from enhanced chemical interjected psychotherapy medicines integrated with the drug of domestic bullying projected distraction, which critical education studies importantly was extracting the catalyst apathy of suffering an inorganic competence to control a lifetime. High School was reminiscent. I remember a favorite part of my senior year; I earned my driver's license at age 18. Though the driving law is 17 in FL. I first earned my permit at 17. I didn't pass the driver's test and written test waiver until I turned an adult 1 year afterwards. My body outgrew intolerant as I become a young adult in my late 20s. God also intervened, as I chose submission. In 2002 when I graduated high school, those times were a cherished flashback picture-perfect memory I immortalized. I had just graduated high school and my biological dad had visited me for the first and last time from NJ down to FL to see me graduate. I was disappointed in a way how his health had also diminished because of the years of him being a chain smoker impacted his lungs. He had stage 4 lung cancer. Another coinciding conditioned he suffered from was a crooked spine that caused him to limp as he walked. My dad wore a chest brace because he had a weak back. He could hardly stand straight with excellent posture disabled in a lot of pain. But when my dad saw me graduate, he poured his tears with a smile in front of me. I gave him a huge hug and told him I loved him. I replied as he conveyed his emotions returned to me, that he loved me as well, and asked for his forgiveness because of the years of childhood abuse he put me through agony of stressful emotional physical injury I dismissed. My father would work 9-5 Monday through Friday coming home exhausted, change his clothes into his robe and pour a beverage of a can of Coke a'Cola alongside with his meal. My mom divorced my father around 1993 when her 1st marriage finalized settlement in a civil court case annulling the marriage cancelled in a civil private hearing. I admit convinced, I was heartbroken my family disconnected, but the writing was on the wall, control and captivity of the marriage, wasn't going to last. During the 1990s, I had supervised visitation to see my dad, but that was temporary. Social Services was ordered by the courts to supervise attention of parent and child conferences monitored by security. My father was playful and regularly cheerful. Before the divorce in the dwelling, he played baseball and other sports with me in the backyard on weekends while my mom cooked dinner. We watched football games together. I remember distinctly he would work long hours to make end's meat cleaning scrap at a local junkyard. But my father wasn't a slouch. He made an honest living in severance pay. He worked despite his repeated offenses of behavior towards the family when he was in a drunken state of Alcoholism. My dad saw me graduate high school, but as I grew up, he wasn't the same father that initiated conflict with me as a minor child. I buried the past. I forgave him so his spirit could finally rest in peace. He passed on 2002-2003. I immediately forgot the past of dwelling circumstantial conflicts. My present instances in confusion for distraction from reaching my staged successes had been confronted clean. I believe an immodest reason I hardly dated was the abuse factor which lead dismay of documented undiscovered domestic crimes. From acts of terrorized abuse in my youth, later in my adulthood, I wanted a tantalizing relationship so much I was affected the repercussions in my later years terrorized spinning drama and trauma from skeptical critics in social culture. If I would marry too young in my 20s, I would probably divorce too young as a father. I would be at a world's end with the ocean falling off into space of a marriage, what I could not control heading into divorce, and a relationship bearing gravity to hold me down trapped into captivity. As I grew older I waited to self-educate wiser. I never married. It's like the factors of early childhood abuse entered another conscientious nightmare contusion that would rehash, because of the irrevocable, irreconcilable, irreducible, and irremediable impact of typical hostility I received from hypocrisy. For the passed 19-21 years 1999 going on to the 2020s and further disestablished heartfelt confidence integrity to have wholesome unity to love together as a family dissolved for a while, until I forgave and forgot. I patched family correspondence. The abuse, domestic violence, tyranny and exposure of judgmental hostility outlasted 2/3s my life. Harassment in the form of surrogate Fascism from my history happened during the high school years unaccounted, conveying published record. The bullying factor impacted infraction in high school increased the catalyst recoil for psychological collision to be diagnosed Bi-Polar 1 disorder with Schizophrenic symptoms. I know what illness I have doesn't weaken me; it charges me in the spirit powerful. The irony experience was through-indifferent stages of crucifixion, conflicting arguments of harassment, and attacks unadjusted of different places in variety forms changed from child to stronger manhood. These were crimes of the beginning millennium 21st century boiling, molding, configuring, reckoning and plotting deceit against me. But by God as my own represented witness striving his humility of defense under his protection, the unprecedented parental abuse, the bullying, the harassment and tyranny from outsider individuals was dissolving. I was justified to make a metaphysical promise, to form an alliance, a connection compromise doctrine with the holy spirit. I communed a deal that what capacity of glad hope I prayed, established a bond with God to keep letting my light be shown, as attacks incited to craft strength, purify might, and survive the horrors of hostile vehement invulnerability sends projectiles of scorn of hurled torture at me in verbal regurgitation. God's offer was saying ***"Son be strong, and show mercy, for in your debt to me in mercifulness you are given sacrifice for revenge, that I will repay what you reap in place of me, you will be given a throne what is thrown at you. My laws will be your judgments returned at your***

adversary because of endless misery. "When my opponent in high school broke my arm during a wresting horseplay standoff in my sophomore year 1999, people displayed friendly contentment in a positive conventionalism. 20 years later, I see that conventionalism disappeared. A few high school chums signed my molded cast and complimented me for my condition to heal. In fact, I was getting flirts from the girls asking me; I was flattered by their mesmerizing charm. But I see 1,2, maybe 3 or less generations away from the extinction of charisma and sympathy because mental health technology for clinical health control analogy is euthanizing a free and state mind of liberty. As I visualize reality, I see a world without empathy and envy for impotence that are helpless from an audience of adolescents that require to be taught moral mannerisms, but don't grow in intelligence toward the light of the world to grow drawing closer their inner-circle towards their goals. We, the flock of God, are pervading away futile in failure because the mindlessness in mind refuse to apologize heartless in heart to forgive, and the soulless in soul reject to reconcile, revolutionizing our co-equal fellow neighbor. Here is some gratitude wisdom. Renounce insubordination and present partnership of unity. It will harmonize a sustainable identity in destiny. There is an unpleasant void negating away at the apple of mankind and its darkening the mind of creation. Adamant justice requires an awakening of battles to clash a universal epidemic, an aberration of evil oppression justice is conquering control of nonconformists. In my senior year of high school, I purchased my year book having proud team-spirit pride for my school that recorded 4-years of programs and activities. All the football, softball, basketballs, baseball, tennis, volleyball state championship games won was documented in my year book for the varsity team girls and boys junior and senior classes. How I wanted to contribute something special in those years, but never postulated the practice of the tryouts ignored, but denied an unprecedented position indicative of the sport's club. I never could escape my shadow of raising my brother, and wouldn't be available to attend practice incessantly expected, when I was controlled and manipulated in the epidemic downfall apocalypse from a controlled dwelling. I could of been a jock, but I wasn't the masculine type with the other macho-guys, until I entered weightlifting in my sophomore year. I went from broader to leaner and meaner in 4-5 months. Took a while, but I bulked up and women were flattered checking me out. I also signed up for weightlifting to harden my bones with muscular tissue regrowth, since the fragment of my left-arm of that horseplay incident involved fractured with a cocky bully. Guidance counselors automatically signed me up for a fitness training program to rebuild me for atrophy-therapy. I wanted to go from zero to hero and never was the adonis of my high school. As I matured, I had a major weight-loss as I developed adulthood. At the end of the year before graduation of high school, was my senior prom. The prom was held at an expensive hotel back in 2002. A lot of spoiled rich ignoramuses attended. They drove $20-30,000 dollars sports cars or inherited down race cars from their parents, even $35,000 drift vehicles and expensive $40,000 racers at that time in the early 2000s late 1990s. In school, I was often surrounded from classmates and other students that came from rich parents and grandparents that were wealthy judges, doctors, lawyers, administrative executives, CFOs and COOs of major fortune 500 business firms heavily progressive in the county. I came from a working class family on the low-end of society that financially made end's meat, that I wanted to fit-in. I was a stranger disassociated downstate with his family on the wrong-side of town, where as an outcast didn't adjust. The prom was a life-time opportunity I never attended. During the time, that event for any constellation, it symbolized the storybook syndrome projected in my situation. I wanted to go to the ball, modeled as example, but I kept confined in control captivity I imagined. It was like drama being imitated psychology locked in a room how the story tells a fairytale peasant girl, but in this situation a male in different circumstances was lectured resentment prohibited from going to the party. I forfeited a memory uncreated and uncared. That's how I felt. I stepped in the storybook shoes. If the shoe fits, that's the one first unprecedented memory in the end to inherit the glory and honor from dejected ridicule by a family in a feudal system of progressivism demonstrated, assessing an analogy. During my previous high school antiquated years end, I, from 2000 to 2003 held a job for 3 years. It was my first job at a fast food restaurant. I saved every penny, every crumb of the cookie, and a dime for a security down payment to buy my first car at 18 years old. In 2002, could be 2003 indecisive to estimate the exact year, I bought a vehicle which was a used 1996 sports 2-wheel drive car. I must of saved 3 years monetary asset security for a car. I had no car payments and never took a loan from a bank with capital working credit interest approved for payments owed. I bought my car in full-working capital owned for 7 years. Those days were glorious and prosperous years, because when I worked and as I worked, I didn't feel controlled, as if, I was on a bequeathed disability system receiving a vehicle bribe check from a 3rd-party inherited. I worked tirelessly in my teen years for cash conversion award granted, the grandeur endeavor of capital enterprise, pure fiscal Capitalism, than being reprimanded tough parental recommendations for fear and control to earn benefits through ubiquitous hard-labor progress simplified in life. I was an upstanding student with no traffic violations or criminal records at that time in high school. I kept the straight, but tough narrow path to climb the corporate ladder of the business in my younger years, as I attended college back in NJ; but as I grew older with the advancement of social media, corporate giant technology, I began to slow down stagnant. I know it sounds that I'm belittled my capabilities that I haven't discovered, but I was initially beginning to underperform in the job setting, underproducing complexity to exercise detail as a tool for exclusive career achievement to compete in the labor market, which would disavow me excellence from an expedience standpoint to conform captive sellable material for any commercialization career. As my 30s approached the disorder of symptoms persisted to grew rampant. My illness diagnosed through the regulation of forced institutionalized pharmacology propaganda. It would delay an inevitable inability to perform certain job duties to connect real workable progress, earning a paycheck to cohere indirect supervision communication, and adhere feedback on a practical platform delivered back general management in the work place. At the time I owned my first car, I was assigned strict rules for safe driving responsibilities. I was mandated a curfew because of school on weekdays. I wasn't allowed to go to parties or people's houses because of the confrontation prevention of drug and alcohol addiction, that never intercepted poisonous inconvenience against my position to paralyze my ego. I wasn't allowed to date because of school and work throughout the week. I barely dated, because I was still under the age of 18, until, I became an adult and purchased my car at the dealership cash deal tax, tag, title factory warranty and insurance was sold to me at the dealership. I was excited. I attributed outstanding pride. I worked hard towards buying my first owned car. Experience nullified a subtle disposition of control and captivity against me in the abusive setting, but it was still ongoing even as I came home from either school or work. I couldn't just enjoy a quiet time spending company with friends or acquaintances in town. I had friends from school I called on the phone.

There were crimes from an incident which took place after school. I followed a bunch of goons into a wooded area that created a fort by the road leading to the campus. It so happens these goons weren't my friends but hooligans, because the way they behaved and projected their conduct towards me was violent bullying. One of them burned my arm with a cigarette lighter. I remember vividly back in 1999. That present time was the only initial point my brother's father, my stepfather, who stood-up to protect me in my advent defense against adolescent teen violence. I was glad he protected me to prevent injury then, because it showed the only time he cared after battling the downfall of his private case. Middle School was nefarious further remembered. I got suspended from school up to 1-week, because I incompetently had a swiss army knife on a key chain connected to my house keys. A student reported me to the principal. What was notified about me was, I had to be sanctioned into detention 1-week. The administrators of the school took the matter seriously outrages, and I knew political propaganda was going to be warranted because someone saw my keys and misacted drama overwhelmingly. I never used a swiss army knife as a weapon. The swiss army knife was a tool. I did a lot of whittling with tree branches as wood crafts to create figures and characters carving for art projects. I was an artist that drew a lot of sketched images of portraits when I attended college, but political propaganda belittled me outrageous progressive judgment toward my position as 1999 closed.

In middle school, from retrospection at a previous time, I brutally finished my Jr. years catastrophically. Last year of middle school in 8th grade, I had a conflict. I was brutally injured by an attacker that punched me in the stomach and in my right eye, where I was almost permanently blinded from bodily damage. I had early termination to leave school for the summer, 1-week prematurely prior before the start of summer. I went to the hospital for treatment of the bleeding. The doctors proscribed medication for pain management. In the old days, I still managed to sustain the glad joy of my spirit endeavored, confidence after a major blowout from a dispute that couldn't stand on its own knees like modeling a table or chair missing 4-legs, or a car without any tires balancing to carry any rest of peace. However what was the worse case scenario that abruptly iterated unprecedented was the frequent vulgar intimidation from my 8th grade Math teacher and his clan of my other classmates in his classroom that harassed me. After I graduated high school my bullying days pacified their disappearance. When I upgraded advancement to high school throughout the years, the genuine bullying egotism pacified. In each surpassing year intellectual, I was forgetting the past, as I continued to master my education grandeur into adulthood. There was 1 particular girl for 4-years of high school admirably I want to discuss, which I was fondly attracted to, and she always made eye contact with me and smiled pleasant. She was in a relationship; however, she still showed interest in me throughout the school years for 4-years from freshman to senior year. She brought to my bright face and curious appeal her caught attention. She had a crush on me like no other girl did, that was initial first crush. In my sophomore year, which was her junior year, I bought her a card and chocolate rose for Valentine's Day as a spiritual moment of memory forever. Now nothing evolved from that point forward ahead. She confronted me automatically, knowing I delivered the Valentine's Day candy and card contents. She was flattered by my prestigious gifts of honor I showered her with that special day love. But vicariously imagined the message is interpreted the old saying that puppy love is a wishful old triumph tale of war and glory disappeared in the wind. She confronted me claiming she had a boyfriend. I took her answer with hospitality and swallowed my pride. I respected her wishes and moved on, but even after she disclosed her marital status, she still demonstrated eye contact and forms of affection by flirting with me like no other girl did in my life. She was flattered by my offer so genuine, even-though she had been taken by someone else. Years passed, and we both graduated. We separated in different years and divided in the totality of 2 distinct disburse lives.

Although I acknowledge I moved on, remembering those happy times recorded in my conscience I use that support tool method system of reminiscence application enabled to identify the amazing scintilla mechanism, necessary to reinstate the old version character of who I am, what I used to be before I aged, and what standards I represent. It's doesn't change who I am or defy my challenges, it remasters them transformed as transparent immaterialism.

CHAPTER 9

INTERNET SCAMS, FAMILY CONFLICT, & ABSENT MARRIAGE

As you learned in recent chapters, returning to Florida had ramifications on my personality and physical strain of character emphatically reiterated. In my worst discretion, I had to heal from wreckage of a body weakened in pain and bodily injury from the implant of chemical-therapy as the years progressed. Being institutionalized pharmacology on psychotropic medication reduced me irregular. I did have a counterproductive negative impact, how I responded to my inability to interpret my competence with friends in my town, and because I had a disadvantage connecting with people they had a greater range of capability skill thinking faster than I did. Being I'm on the psychotropic medicines stops the neuron from conflicting my regular thought process, I record notes and understand I stagger in my 30s now, than-even when I was 18. I can't evidently substantiate enough the medicines wore me immobile, but the side-effects of what I experienced are a good indictor of my weakness adamant orders forced, were taken from doctors and the subversive ultimatum of parental control. Medicine side-effects interfered with my work habit, prevented me from writing or working consistent to vulnerable strain, restricted me from being creative for putting things together, distorted me in fear, and disengaged me from accomplishing goals in the worst case narrative possible. I reject the disgrace how far-left progressive pharmaceutical companies distribute psychotropic medicines like pieces of candy, restraining innocent people stressful who are victims as patients, than the dignity title *Americans* misconstrued mentally-ill misused instead of applying the characteristic term "***behavior wellness***." In fact conscious studies found the psychotropic medicines weaponizes the behavior actions of the victim to react disorderly. I once read an article in a medical magazine where lobbying state medical officers reverse the order of the patient's intelligence, sabotaged, what they are diagnosed from medical examiners' research. The information practitioners discover from their reports for the pharmaceutical companies is granted clearance what is mandated by court judges. The mandate undermines methods to force their patients on the compound agent. Studies found the agents absorbs or incorporates adrenaline to respond sadistic subordinate behavior and submissions solicitous crimes, the victim aggressively opposes the sleeping affects of the dehumanized performance of the weaponized antidepressants, forcing a person to subtly appear deranged or psychotic, when the case appears, is he or she is confused disturbed fading asleep, when on the compound. Changing the subject, there are various-versions of archetype forms of technology. Surely there would be cures to alternative treatments of pharmacology studies and research on a regular month to month basis per-year for care, instead of dangerously pumping adverse chemicals into the brain with side-effect symptoms to diminish people's conditional performance developed; especially than, exemplified experiments affects lab rats what correlation damages innocent victims. Liberal statism overruns and overrides the opinion decision independence of the American spirit, of, when, and suppose purposely you're contained in the correctional system. In my experience there has been minimal liberty of free choice being controlled captivity monitored institutionalism 2/3s my age from internal damages a lifetime. Medical health tyranny from its surrogate *"Psychiatric Fascism"* uses cunning diagnosis controlling methods, descended from doctors' practice that persuades families, ultimately convinced inferior, that someone has to be medicated according to officials, omitted the input of my own self-decision. Then all became history beneath rehabilitation, as I was subjected to the science of progressive subversion. There were multiple factors of slave-like mistreatment indoctrination through chores or either work and rent for room and board, which I volunteered to assist enhancing the case of having a place to stay while paying my rent. I would wash kitchen dishes in the details with my rent, working while living where I stay. I didn't mind, but care getting some assistance participated, contributing shared respect to do chores aside with me in the manner of the dwelling in good conscience. I had no place or apartment to rent with prices out of my affordability range. For 2/3s growing-up, because of inept joblessness, my incompetency of behavior health component-conflict determined by state licensed doctors, my records, evidence of tests, written reports delivered, submission facts of counter-conflict against my will, the position of being a patient than a decent Conservative American restrained on recessive counterproductive psychotropic anti-mood stabilizers while I was suddenly dwindled decompensation of my condition, eroded myself bodily injury internal damage in the long-run I did have a disability that kept a cruse following me. I was essentially raised as a beta-male than the alpha-male adonis. So I realized had a broken mind discouraged; I was disheartened, because the progressive premise of the progressive way methods the baby boom generation strict-toughness raised the generation Z and millennial generation would inclusively filter specific adults celibate further restricted from dating, marriage, and continuing their descendants to populate generations beyond. When I was at the state hospital during the time ordered into my hospitalization 2016, the forensic team constituted a disagreement that just because there was a fault in my behavior health, doesn't mean it would impact my dating relationship platform. But, I debunked their conclusion of facts, because the factors were prevalent. Where I was, I was subjected to being confronted revealing devastating details which carried embarrassment to my condition. I couldn't date or experience the reality of enhanced exquisite intimate performance. Knowledge-acknowledged that as I grow older its more difficult to meet someone single in my generation unmarried, who could be appalled hearing haunting shadows from my past encounters of trouble would resist a relationship, chastise me, or could breakup. Still, I'm grateful God restored my power of understanding, my capacity of knowledge, my ability to assess thought. I do yield, I would like to get married and have a family of my own someday, without the further bombardment controlled crimes of family progressive tyranny suffered through and throughout the years, striping my political stripes of stifling liberty. I trust in the changes of my wellness. The insurgency of trauma impacted me bad experience for years in shock, which outplayed me an egregious imbecile, caused me to lose several jobs. The progressive ridicule intimidation from family drama-trauma of troubles of ultra-intolerance was a narcotic that didn't help, but it didn't heal either, only hurt as why I became permanently disabled today. Supremacy forms of totalitarian-psychiatric embolism surrounding pharmaceutical parapsychology is a mind-bending, mind-altering, and heart-breaking action in the splinter's mind of general, atypical, liberal progressivism. Behavior Health facilities distributing the psychotropic derivative by doctor's prescription are only investigated state-level jurisdiction by law according to every state's standard version of state health inspectors from the state's public health department for documentation, report, and conclusion of facts. I researched the medications I've been mandated to take upon compliance. Through the thorough fading phase of 9 years seldom, I can express, it's a basic step-up upgrade than having respiratory arrest from the compound un-quelled since I couldn't breath. However, there are neurotransmitters that have to be calibrated regular stabilization of control by pumping oral medication by day to be alert, focused, maintained proper, and self-controlled. That gets complicated to voluntarily contribute anything an effort to a group, a community, a city, a state or country to be productive. I never intended to be on anti-depressants. 1% out of 99.9% of the time I'm not depressed being off them. The anthesis is opposite I oppose. Through modern day parental oligarchy from the science of subversion, parental progressivism tricks the generations of young adults to submission under a criminal conspiracy, that, people by the time they are young adults have a disorder beneath the drunken influence of excessive concern to discredit their ability to function, enforcing a statist question by distorted example to keep consistently compressing the narrative *"Are you okay?"*, *"I'm concerned about you."* or *"What's wrong? "You seem to be sad."* The parent is inspecting their children's egos as a goal to compress inquisition to suggest clinical study for suggestive concern there could be an inability to clarify a cohered disorder present for unapparent treatment that is pushed necessary. That idea is exactly subjected how Liberal Fascism works, which is a fundamental organized Berlin Germany style habit conformed to the occupation of American clinical Sciences of enteral medicines. It is necessary which is why innocent Conservative Americans are being diagnosed falsified disorders under the influence of forced psychotropic activity according to their assigned doctors, due to medical terrorism, essentially psychiatric terrorism. It controlled the mass population of Western Europeans in hostile genocide WWI and WWII with beginning and ending dates July 1914-2019 and September 1939-June 1945 of the 2nd Western-European wars combined from the deception antiquation of crime, control, and captivity. Then discourse capitalized and institutionalized sanitarium clinics pervaded undertone of left-leaning Fascist descendants transmigrated to America undisclosed. The radicals adapted dynamics of their hostile agenda in the branches of politics through decades of pop culture and the activism movements of the 1960s, which modeled an example to other victims, innocent circumstances being captured in captivity of the criminalized progressive spider's web. Unlimited reason wasn't an antidote inconsiderable in my family's long-run thorough drama. Reason should always be a formula for compassion and self-control, and as comfort not compromise through any exception to complexity. I have prayed and demonstrated humility towards hypocrites as the years changed and coalesced with my universe joined with their different universe, while times were getting better. I showed maturity and rationality diffused avoiding to being lectured ethics and etiquette from my parent(s). I never had to be mistreated violently, because unlike being identified indistinguishable raised special, I had an underdevelopment. I learned by watching, listening, hearing, learning, and capable of adapting observant confined skill increased to my intelligence with convinced confidence. There was absolute no absent reason, while rationing the ability to exert reasonable characteristics I had to be forced to behave. I was a quick studier and learner underestimated. What slowed me down was the torture received. As I notated in the previous chapters of this book, I might of missed or stated the pointers of my dating culture reality of my social life settling with my ex-girlfriend. I'm white, straight, heterosexual, God-trusting male by normal standardized preference on a permanent basis that's attracted to caucasian women and don't wish to conform the crime, control and captivity of identity politics by force. Times have transformed, but the customs and traditions that shaped and molded mankind are irreplaceable. They will always be subjected accountable. I have stayed mostly single since college. In the corporate tech-giant gateway world, government is advancing their strategy for people encountering their partnerships to meet online rather authentic, which I find synthetic than genuine in person. I was an innocent victim of identity theft of 2014. I was 1 out of 24 million financial consumers of banking information that was inexplicably-exploited by cyber-hacking reported by the national media. Roughly 2006 for 15 years, I have been played for a fool talking to a scammer from Nigeria thinking it was a gorgeous model, who bluntly conned me mislead, into thinking, I was communicating to the person in the picture, but wasn't her. The girl in the photograph, who I thought was the person online, was incongruent. I was an ignorant fool naive at the time. As a young man my age, I had to play it safe because these online criminals having been operating for about 20-40 years with advanced evolution of technical data procession upgrades to internet technology. I dislike dating sites because of the particular potential risk of jeopardizing my identity to theft, cyber-hacking and even being a victim of being scammed. These scammers are professionals using cutouts of models from exotic centerfold magazines from Vegas in their profiles and changing their names frequent, blatantly smooth-talking their devious blunt tantalizing methods to lure young guys, thinking, that they are talking to beautiful models in the pictures to steal hundreds of thousands of dollars and overdraft their bank accounts empty. On a frequent basis these online bandits are shutdown by federal agencies by a protection anti-criminal agency that work to protect your identity, other times not because of inadequate submission of limited evidence produced. These online criminals cleverly don't always leave a paper trail to be caught auspiciously, so cleverly know, they are are being monitored by federal law enforcement agencies. Doing my years of research of being a victim to scams, I intelligently and methodically had to put on the conscious mask of the inspector and get inside of the mind of the criminal, ask lots questions that would voluntarily lead me to the right answers to strengthen myself, since a victim of scams. I had to grow skillfully wiser to distribute a diligent message to help other victims incorporate intelligence to be protected. In retrospection looking back, because of the immoral activity that caught up to me, I was immature to get married and have a family once I got out of college. I internally felt ungrateful, because I would see the integrity of other guys around me in my generation, my age, getting married and having children in their mid-20s early 30s settling down of the case. I was still raising my brother a full-time role-player, putting on the role of a surrogate father raising him. I strongly believe 1/3 of my life raising my brother stole the denominator attention of having my own marriage and offspring. I learned respect and honor with dignity towards the territory, but I felt I was being tested my liberty with liability. I felt stereotyped-responsibility of someone else's deliberate irresponsibility forced upon my goals suppressant of indifferent situations. Sometimes I'd often felt rejected in an argument, which would lead to a dispute in the form of psychological verbal abuse from an emotional meltdown of withdrawn characters. I can guarantee, I would not be in the scuffle of rippling trauma, the money-pit of despair for prosperity, if my first book The Blue Sphere was a major popular success invention. I took a gander at writing my first literary book and know realistically there was no actual way, I would become a titled dwelling name in the talent industry overnight, through periods of practice and credit. But in my truest personality discouraged it was a new novel, a new invention, and brand new superhero premise I introduced to the 21st century that had an anti-climax continuation. My first novel was going to perpetuate the promise satisfaction of a comic book sequel. The Blue Sphere wasn't elected a best seller novel. My career path had been blundered. I had been forced poor through cunning manipulation of gradual deceit. The Blue Sphere received poor ratings, reviews, and grade in quality book inspection when accommodated by judges of major book clubs in America. I did receive responses of constructive criticism, but obligated to do a relaunch when revisions to the book is rereleased, reaching a density bubble to my audience, a remastered edition republished despite a population attempting to defuse rejection in a counterculture. The psychodramatic antics of being on mandated psychotropic stagnation lethargically wore down my writing, tired my activities, underproduced testosterone secretion, and has had a revolutionized defect process of drowning my chances of being part of the alpha-male wolf pack, but instead isolated in the beta-male sheep dinner fenced through practiced policy assessments of clinicians. Let's contemplate a fact. I failed to deliver my goals, because I had guilt not to escalate above a higher enough foundation of a my grace-given returned faith of my faults, rejected to stipulate all the glory returned to Jesus Christ. Delay was another pointer for excuse, while meeting deadlines exiled my weakened condition. I believe, because of the indescribable oppression I underwent being overwhelmed compressed under dwelling authority with a strict family, that underestimated my God-given talents growing up in the length of time. It lead to the underdevelopment process. But, I didn't go to Jr. college to be a bum years later on a socialized disability system. I wasn't raised in poverty undereducated or uneducated and to write 2 books to be poor a destitute. That's not the case, but to profit largely that would have expanded reinvestment and taxes payed for forthcoming future literary premised pieces of worked book titles. When I was in college I felt beneath disrespect under control and captivity when I was picking my classes for college. The specialist was persuading me what field required I should major in generally. I told her of course acting, the performing arts as a major than an elective. My mom convinced me there is no way of making a paycheck in that industry unrecognized because of the 1% estimated goal of getting noticed by popular demand. She was intellectually virtuous by inclined wisdom. I was in letdown mode of sorrow and grief dissuaded to take Computer Animation and Graphic Arts for a lifetime career. I didn't want to major into something, that I knew, I was going to have meet deadlines with reasonable cause, and wasn't going to finish on time, which scrutiny was going to translate reprehensible to my disadvantage, but that's realistic. Because I wanted to chose acting as my major rejected my planned decision unconvinced, I was in let-down mode disappointed. But now that I'm older, I wish I had gone to a secondary college to achieve my Bachelor's degree in Communications.

I like writing, expressing the truth, corresponding journalism in a self-explicit newspaper with transparent facts for delivering statements of a driving message in cultural current affairs; where, I don't stereotype people's opinions, just commutate facts to let the audience read their own private unopened mail of details. There is a huge medium for journalism with a start wage researched at $36.26 per hour and a message to elaborate about the crimes pervading in America from the emboldened untold press that are being blacklisted unkept secret from unsought truth of audiences' eyes of witnesses, those getting the information viably unrevised without outspoken agendas. So because the entertainment industry is fading, disappearing, dying, there is a medium advancement of opportunity demand to incline hiring journalists that: assess, identify, estimate, establish and verbalize accountability of facts needed being held captive from criminalized opponents in the press corps. I would still have to make deadlines in an oped editorial where inquiries of indicative questions are being asked, what I would be responsible as a journalist to do to ascertain answers. I see the intolerance and egotism from a side of millennial disposition that does bellicose vacuous vitriol of attacks against the family-raised caucasian male. Identity politics displays a character element of moral integrity sincerely gone in a disarray. Occasionally instigation outplays drama in criminalized hatred, the harassment from fundamentality ridicule, which has changed the culture and generated an epidemic of insolent-isolation in the dating mechanics gone to disrepair. Its system changed the millennial decaying culture. Faith and wisdom to be given an opportunity by grace rests on compromise of a miracle. I was the product of an outcast experiment social program growing up, why I was the unpopular-broken-merchandise band of misfits. I did everything according to the rules of society, the policies of forced institutionalism, the breakdown criteria of being raised in a decent family and had my despair of pitfalls, that I had to resurrect-recovery restoring reputation to my good name and earnest character. It wasn't me. I worked hard thoroughly on a 2nd major assigned book deal in support of the other book and successfully aspired a national book review of 9.68% best selling book nomination of a motivational Philosophy tool book. I had limited literary representation, but still smiled, as I move forward aggressively in victory winning. I had my goals, my fortunes, my desire and everything excluded to be recognized more achieved aspired in showbiz gone from the socialized crimes of captivity. I obeyed in the subordinate military industrial complex dwelling breath beneath the skin of hostile argumentativeness, that today with half a blemished disfigured face partly healed, the physical injuries that impaired the capacity of my mental capabilities, controlled by regular med-management therapeutics, had torn me down emboldened of judgment. I still retain contentment of my soul without its dismissal absence. I'm conscious in a believable conscience, I still incorporated the witness of the divine-nourishing and pleasant-life-watering spirit. The world of family is like a 2-sided mask. One side of the mask is criticism with elements of Authoritarianism and the other side is the world with control of Fascist-Communism, where there are empty sides remaining to celebrate liberty. Then the mask is lifted off the face and you see the whole picture of the person free in the will of personified prominence---prospered. I'm that type of Conservative that justifies belief as the advancement of government science evolves technology, you have to marry critical-thinking to know everything pervasive. People can't be forced to marry government bureaucracy. It involves allegorical critical thinking every time. Americans on a consistent basis are being subjected a vehicle integration from suggestion for inquisition to the superior cybernetic catalyst upgrade next stages of of human biology, as a transposition working disorder is efficiently taking place in the matter of crime, control, and captivity to repurchase an underclass of slavery. Government regulation impairs labor stagnant to integrate things together and be creative. Anyhow, I matured throughout the months and years since my family drama. I adjusted to harmony. I reconciled peace and asked for forgiveness, through God to stand with him, for him, follow him, and in him. Because if you don't forgive others, as half you forgive yourself, you don't forgive yourself as a complete whole system without the other parts yourself to forgive your opponents, granting that deputized forgiveness in richness of character to forget the mistakes and disputes of the recent years passed in pity controlled under captivity. There are things I could have accomplished not gone to waste for mischief like I did, that I repent, and grew wiser with a sense of instinct and morality from senseless acts of trouble. I know, I'm imprisoned for life under the influence of physical and chronic psychotropic-pharmacology and persuasiveness; it will not eagerly withdraw me out of institutionalized clinical studies of experimentation. I have a disorder noted in my records, that the redundant disorder behind the curtain of transparent pretenses inexplicably perpetuates its manufactured performance as I stay stabilized on the chemical compound indoctrination for years to descend. My dysfunction persisted with the medicine forced to ingest on permanent basis. The treatment fueled injury to my situation. My health was coping an emotional state of turmoil drama, suffering from malignant personality in decline. Others in manner of this subject could doubt my story as a conspiracy, inconclusive rejection of invalid facts, but I'm also documenting what I personably saw and witnessed, what my body and mind also experienced verifiably in my book that parental agitation was an engine of progressive authoritarian techniques through my upbringing. Unilateral control of criminal conceit acted coercion in a variable way to undermine my own decisions of reconciliation; especially, having the capacity to judge knowledge clearly and clarify prudent choices not to mortify a counter-conflicted community insurgency. I, like the other 1% of the Bi-Polar 2.3 million Americans are victims of the Industrial Military Pharmaceutical Patient Engineer Complex or *I.M.P.P.E.C.* It's a symbolism as the *ICBM* of oral or injection nuclear medicine, that wore me down the concept of be addicted conformed to anti-depressant compound medicines indefinitely, mandated to be ingest by mandated psychiatrists' proscribed orders a lifetime through clinical trial control studies. I believe, had I not been forced on oral medications from childhood to adult estimated 60% near under 2/3s, I suspect, I wouldn't be encountering indifferent scenarios of difficult tasks to perform; such activity enervated doubling the impact of hostile abuse layered suffered as the results. There's been a series of practical reviews of my condition identified and evaluated, but excluded of disarrangement of coerced facts between partnership of behavior wellness partners, that which I unaccounted for have been positioned in a technicality in a produced a misfortune agenda. I want to label something retrospectively that I could have made a timely decision that could have altered the destiny of my unfortunate circumstance path I'm in. Back in high school in the final class of my senior year I had a Algebra. However, before I registered for this class I had the option of taking a military cadet recruiter training course class essentially. Thinking back, I regret taking Algebra and not this military cadet recruiter training course class. What advantage aspect would I use number throughout the history of my life that involves problem solving, computation, simplification and evaluation? None because had I had taken this military cadet recruiter training course class I would been delegated mannerism of respect, self-control, patience, obedience, strength, integrity and endurance. I would have favored wanting to go into the military, but because genetically I have a neurological electrochemical imbalance disorder, typically, I would not be approved for the military background screening examination process to be enlisted for training and assignment as a CO for special operation. Thinking back vigorously pragmatic, I seriously gave unquestionable grief of all the opportunity vehicles I missed. But I had less of a disadvantage. I was younger and didn't get the run-around from jobs, deadlines of my books, obligated college classes to finish, personal conflict at home and community issues. My health in the late 90s early 2000s was vibrant; I would have want to engulf the benefits of joining the military to honorably serve my nation for freedom. I would have lost a limb or my life; or, I would have came back wounded guaranteed a lifetime pension from the government a hero, and had been documented in the history books in the blood I shed in the battlefield a dream never saw its dawn of birth to admission. However, I've been civilian all my life that went the opposite route which took longways to excel a Jr degree and a state license education course career certification degree of excellent boundaries I had to cross. The entertainment industry can either be insanity or fantasy to those that pay and play role to clime its ladder. A crucial job without any top-level college degree requirement is a longer process that's harder to achieve for myself, through durable workload activity; that, should I change my attitude, I must endeavor effort of heart and righteous intellect to deliver accurate results able by climbing a steeper mountain in the afflictions addressed.

CHAPTER 10

RESTORED IN CHRIST, FAITH AND CONCLUSION

I had already been forgiven, since my 2-times visited Jail 2010 and 2015. My groundbreaking forgiveness came through rehabilitation and co-equally re-engaging familiar workforce habit for a limited time, before claimed legal disability status by the state. On October 11th, 2010, as vividly remembered, I had an out-of-body near death experience. I had an encounter, where I visited the other side of purgatory. There, in a place was my aunt and grandmother waited, just as a I remembered them, when they died 3 months between apart in 2009 reinvigorated.

I was in a field. There were trees high as the California redwood sequoias. Behind me was a 50-100 foot waterfall and a river subsequent leading into a lake. I gave my aunt a hug and my grandmother beside them. My grandmother padded my back and then I felt myself being dragged backward behind by my silver cord, being tugged into my body, departing the other-side. After I woke-up from my near death experience I was short of breath temporarily. My heart was beating fast, but I began to control my condition back to normal after rehydration. I was alive, but amazed since making an apparent conscious-connection to my loved ones deceased. My faith skyrocketed and grew stupendous. I immensely was in the holy spirit and gave my entire submission---surrender to God. I basically underwent a transparent OBE condition for the first time explained details communicated by modern day parapsychology science-fiction experts discuss on paranormal surreal talk shows. My short-comings of inactions became more confident addressing the problems, and confronting them with the glory of Christ. My encounter with my deceased aunt and grandmother was a message addressed to me that I was not alone. They were with me and I have my *Armor of God* equipped against the totality fear of uncertainty moving forward. 2010 and 2015 were predicaments, because both years were times revisited, where I was at a local Naples homeless shelter, on my own during a self-contained limited period of responsibility to survive, pay rent, work, eat, and keep busy. On the foundation basis of my legal drama twice, I had restraining order not to contact my family at home 1-2 miles distant of town. I prayed with others, and myself in solitude determined with fortitude to restore my dignity. I prayed silent in my mind having a conference with God, asking Christ, *"what is it you're clarifying me to do? What do you need me to do? I know you sent me on a mission into the wilderness to teach me a lesson, so, I can preach the ministry of the gospel in a sense, for a good format, of the carried word you are using me as a vessel for disciplines."* The less I talked, the more I inclined my ear to listen to the word of God, turned into knowledge and made use of the useful tool of God's plan from his law written in his book of life to gain enormous commission quality of salvation. I wanted to be an agent of change instead of an agent of despair or an agent of blame. Today I'm reliable to help, calmer from clamor, and transfigured. Let me be honest. We have all heard the term *"be a victor of outcome not a victim of circumstance." **Be a defier of difficulty, instead, deficient a defeatist.*** But God sees the truth and test the hearts of men to those that are called to his name in salvation. So Christ wants us to also be a warrior of war not a worrier to wear out. Because if we wear out subtly, so soon or suddenly, we lose grip of control over personality, contentment, confusion and concentration to function our character to protrude equal stability shared with the unity out of the solidarity of our enemies. I often talk of salvation, but even if we call out the name of Jesus Christ emphatically, are we really saved through the free gift of grace without pulling our own gravity of work incorporated by supervision of our superiors? What satisfaction gain of quality, or, moral skill can we achieve any inspired goal without building material and integrating things together by work integrity to accommodate our needs, and for others to be judged salvation required to be approved by God? Christ must feel our work justified than seeing. If we build the material with soul of the immaterial, just easily, it facilitates effort efficiently to assemble elements of innovated wisdom devised. God will discern our souls blossomed with worth of the holy spirit capable of salvation. Fruitful salvation must be accomplished by built grace through gravity of insight patented with intelligence thoughtfully processed. It isn't free to earn. We must work our way to harmony faithfully. My early teens was productive, but mid-adulthood, I became stagnant as from a psycho---pharmacology crisis shock sluggishly curbed my impairment from the Bi-Polar I disorder. Both disorder and impaired disability has disallowed me to express my difficulties and hurdled my challenges taken obligation forefront to address my story modeled in dynamic premise through faith. When the wind of ages come, I would miss lost the younger years when I would actually receive an appealing cure. I never stop diligently fighting for the truth. If your absent withheld licensed truth without God's grace, you're still controlled-captive half a person and not a whole person freed. Throughout the years the happiness of my family's spirit quieted the light of bright contentment. The fire dimmed bleak even commenting any iota reference with respect to my integrated relationship of God; it upset my opponents and fueled a sparked argument debunked debates that offended conflict. I think in contemporary situations, because of the modern millennial deficit-impact-defect globally with not returning to church or relinquishment joining social groups to heal, so hope can be shared, being the essence of prosperity has declined. Everyday I'm battling fear and paranoia even with the medical derivative compound substances forced control captive, not to be fearful and terrorized by the militant mentality of secular evasive silence. Unfortunately, I was given that certain malcontent evident reprogrammed sponge-washing treatment. Is it a conspiracy what the government is doing to my generation and upcoming generations? Am I being a corporate product of big techno-pharmacology, where, insurance contractors are making billions of dollars off of my mind and health from the anatomy of my body? Individual consumers' health are at risk by artificial performance of careless and mindless medical treatment for greedy profit. When I was younger, as a child, I had a cat named Snickers. I felt secured safe; peaceful and courageous, because I had owned property that I could love. Although it was an animal, she was an organic living-breathing life-form I could love, which could return love back. I had Snickers for about 9-10 years. My family and I had to disown her, because she kept sneezing. Snickers was older, getting sicker. She was shedding dander. Snickers could hardly breath right. The family was inducing the dander prone to allergies. We sold her to another tenet that gladly bought her, and would take care of her ill condition, until one day unannounced, she died unexpectedly of old age. I estimate assumably unaware when she died, it's when I moved out of the state. That was the last time I would see Snickers alive before high school graduation, relocating back to New Jersey. I loved Snickers so much, I embellished the position of being a first time dad. However the irony is, she was an animal and not a child. If I were to get a substitute replacement pet, years later I would own a dog, because I never owned a dog subsequent. I want a loyal friend that's playful; I can return a friendly gesture of sincerity where I would be responsible for taking care of its needs. In my memoir, I'm enthusiastic to overlook retrospection of my past in detail the disputed mistakes and examine the strengthens that occurred up to this point, now that my spotlight has been written. I enjoy sharing cultural events that happened and aspire to keep practicing my goals, never forfeiting the trials determined to surmount incredible inclusion of challenges I have faced everyday. Turning to Christ revolutionized my character into the unimaginable recovered man granted. Being unable to be work-abled and work-minded, coincided often unpleasant being on disability. Bills had to be paid. While my faith awakened, I share it performing stagnant; I kept it private. God is detailing, configuring, arranging, itemizing, reversing, and revising parts and points for new goals of destiny for my future. An ultimate change in a manner of meaningfulness purpose must be mustering a better optical aspect signature career for business success planned. I remember the fun days when my relatives and family would gather for the holidays, or special occasions creating fond memories shared. There's always a lot of pride, but virtue lacking. Patience is either inexistent or an underperformed circumstance. It takes deep-thought communication to establish sincerity for a reconnection in the family, that would cope with the frustration for deep-seeded emotions of genuine personality. I have more secured humility and respect in my actions towards others, my work performance, and kindness to disciple a stranger, than I do in my thoughts. The thoughts take longer to process the ingenuity of integrity because of my diagnosis, which is why I have an endless deficit to assess my thoughts for shuffling my speech through hardship understanding. You don't need an expert to evaluate judged facts. But I'd say pharmacology med-manipulation excluded the pervasive indispensable-inclusion of thorough-research, drastically overwhelmed me rundown inefficient of dramatics, to control captive my masculinity and stamina locked government mandate. I couldn't prohibit tenacious bodily function breakage from child to adult. I remember a reminiscent-precedence, when I was in jail and received a Christmas card from my aunt up in New Port Richie FL. It specifically self-spoke a message with the except *"you must put your total trust surrendered back to the Lord and take up faith with him."* I contemplated the meaning of that message what my aunt commented. I kept my grace astute positioned with God. I had to keep strong-minded and headstrong, because I was in a detention center identified with culprits of broken-down harden criminal history around Naples. Some individuals made poor life-choices in the correctional system. A few inmates were in lockup because of drug offenses and majority were repeated offenders. I had to keep quiet and mind my business, patiently getting through the 1-year jail sentence for the 2nd offense I committed at home back October 22nd, 2015 I briefly stated in the beginning of my initial biography. I flushed my bad attitude and omitted reckless character flushed down the toilet, putting and exerting inspiration--- intentionally to march forward back on track, meditating on my aunt's words written in the Christmas card. The words were a well-needed antidote provided, the cure to restore balance louder on a lonely heart alienated away from my family for the 2nd time returned to Naples, since the first crime Sept. 2nd, 2010, blossomed rehabilitation. My battle wasn't over with the unaccomplished desire to obtain success from a failed book deal or outrage from an altercation with my family. I unrecognizably delayed intelligence to identify a powerful enemy that held me captive, while I failed attempt to confront the conflict stronghold of evil, than, while evil was bullying me captive upon contact. I didn't carefully discern a composited factor notation of the time the culture concurred against me in a difficult compromise. I was writing a book at a time I didn't have a literary manager. I didn't have a marketable vehicle of goal of approach method of management of organized planning established. It was my first book, at the time, I was compulsive during those years in the family, that overwhelmingly counteracted competition in and out the outskirts of the dwelling. Politics and an identity of toxic---cultural influence overpowered the comprehensive science modeled art of my work, which is incompatible with a millennial generation. I've often examined how the entertainment setting produces engines of disturbing secular element design---desired in their projects, and perhaps because my work, was more on a positive foot comfortable on a lighter-side, academia doesn't fit the shoe on the foot of their business narrative. I also listed, how because of the emphatic overload of stress waged war on my health, I mismanaged tedious steps to sleep, suffering from endless fatigue. I was overworking days and nights to write an epic novel for my audience. I fell into my own misery trap. The project fell flat because valid facts, my first novel wasn't awarded a showcase display nomination with any major book outlet store dealer. The novel rejected book sale reports in the explanation of reason confronted unquestionable dispute of withdrawing appeal for The Blue Sphere. When you slip and fall, you get back on the horse, so you can relearn from previous experience to circumspect adversity. My devotion to my faith has been a recourse prevented risk assessment---management not to be a repeated offender of error by chance. I would take scripture, writing holy philosophical words down in a journal entry. I would meditate and study an excerpt message with the Lord in translation---attributing a held conversation, rendering a particular message and waiting for the holy spirit to direct me on what he needed me to do to behave, to be forthright in contributing to my family. I would have to cope-cooperating with a rightful attitude, and working eagerly with an enlightened weight unloaded off my shoulders, than the aspect illusion of the mythological Atlas as burden and ruin compressing me a coping mechanism. I didn't want to fall and fail anymore, noted-worthy for my etiquette. I wanted to rise from the darkest shadows of indignity, worthy of achievement, to benefit sunshine of moral accomplishment. I have the mannerisms and spirit to lead like a reborn king. I feel as I was born a slave, but contemplate as a glorified king ordained in the presence of God, despite the crimes, control and captivity of particular tortured-trauma I underwent. I can one day flashback and forget the drama happened gone rising above with justice, empathy, and radiance of the Lord's glory, because I have received salvation already ministered in his name justified. In a dream, I believe credulously I would have the makings and strong bloodline of a king, to empower the powerless self-conscious in riddance of infliction---admonished as I was, who practices redemption for victims obliged to it, are in the despair of oppression avid to be free in liberty, and no longer compounded by the irrepressible torture of any state, government, or darkened kingdom. This indicator is why I self-speak so softheartedly with eloquence dedicated with honesty. A king must judge nations with integrity, grant pardon of salvation given the congregation to a people free and state, restore order and love to regular civilization under the courtship of God, and must understand to protect the sacred trust and values of the laws of the land descended of his people's kingdom. I suppose it's only a dream, foretelling a story of a fulfilling destiny about myself because of the scars, wounds, injury, pain, and misery of transgression which I encountered. I justify aspiration people will vindicate me instead of vilifying me, significant for my past disputes confronted in my present necessary to be revered again. Accepting my character preference now, than before, isn't my final stop ahead. The best outstanding treatment declared an opportunity reconciled for me is possible God requires me to pursue an auspicious career, study his untranslated message, follow the signs and signals of his laws and be obedient for the stewardship in his name. All I asked from Christ, to receive for my abuse, for carrying my version punishment of the cross, because of his bearing name, was to have the co-equal reward as others in hard productive labor and be championed attention smiled with honor. I thoroughly remarked how when you buy something you should get the totality convenience of what you pay. I believe supposedly, I have bought grace under the surrendered submission of God and received convenience for what I have payed. I have payed the price, too much, for hostile displacement from the crimes of dwelling control. I would undergo ridicule of resentment expressed. I would cry lonely nights, silent, believing of the unprecedented retrospection arguments of the past, when, I lived on my own alone in my own apartment, and this is a valid shattered defect I was in disrepair circumstance that required contemplated maintenance. The proscription drug factor by Pharma ineffectively regulates forfeited balance. Med-Maintenance aids incoherent stagnation to mirror me woozy, dopy, sleepy, moody, and whacky. I couldn't conduct performance to be active to be a creative person. When I was at the state hospital in 2016, *I contested the content* I would be on from a magistrate ordered done in med-management hearing. I had a weak case, as a case with a table that had no legs left to stand on. I entered a plea. I had no representation in relationship to my case for defense identity wisdom of knowledge for basic health supplements, minerals or vitamins useful for behavior health treatment, was denied by absolute arbitration rendered by the magistrate in court. Side-Effects of the medication have become addictive to my body, where I have become deficient to resist the occupational coping power of overwhelming toxicity. In previous subsections of this book, I referenced the controlling-condition factor of chores I did in the house. Ever heard of the term opponent-piracy? opponent-piracy is when and opponent behaves like a pirate in a place, zone or area infringing on your rights and self-choice responsibilities indisputable against your liberties in the setting violated. Often there is a penalty of privacy breached. The case is relevant in the community I experienced in FL certain frequent instances. I would be the sole person isolated in chore duty to wash dishes, without blunt sympathy of getting other individuals of the dwelling to assist when kindly asked. The millennial cultural today is a constant insensitiveness display of ridicule in shattered hope for reconciliation from resentment, but the character of others unusual is undesirably irritating from senses being intruded, that there is an evident psychosis of Liberalism. As a far-right Conservative, I have stood my cold shoulder defense of restricted control in the community dwelling. The Liberalism I have encountered has been dangerous. Senseless Liberalism

I have succumbed has been a foul-ball aspect in a major league game for penalty consequence without disqualifying lost points refused to be removed. There's an illegitimate point of satisfaction displeasure in return. The crimes and captivity of Liberalism, from constant behavior opponents has been unpleasant in a strange warped impact of a twilight debacle coma my part for my demeanor. In wreckage, I have been discombobulated subject overexposure far from too much progressive regulation. My story implausible has been about torture from Liberalism, but it has also been battling surreal poignant attacks from the emotional breakage of an unaccountable communist insurgency. I'm not playing the victim card, but have been tortured as a victim for years behind the iron curtain of what's really happening through practical aspects of clinical mandated procedures, reminders, updates, policy changes, practices, appointments and unorthodox performances periodically. America is also a republic of Constitutional liberty, integrity, humility and should be freedom with alienable obligation. When you turn 18 of age the government owns you. What solution is there to mediate a predicament to mitigate, when control is a tool to demoralize and degrade the character or ordinary men and women, developing under the wings of progressivism enforcing strict draconian policy? Liberalism is a destructive force of debunked anti-sociology to force the lucid terror of statism. Statist control and statist attitude has become apparent. Its crimes that I've confronted for 36 years, through wrongful mistakes, disputes, isolated accidents were consequences---subsequent that followed the unprecedented role against my case by derision of opponents, for example, it transferred a generation---genealogy to the other hereditary generations in the schools, the media, and books. History has been either rewritten or misinformed the innocent underprivileged person nullifying their ability to configure their own research, to question the impossible of escaping vital control of Authoritarian traditions. Had I known enlightened---intelligence of the culture, years prior, than ironic to what I know now, I would have wrote my Biography first novel The Blue Sphere for hopeful achievement afterwards. The entire expectation memoir enticed in writing has been explicably---explained toward bold expectation in this book. I wanted to foreshadow examples, elements, and model entity of psychological situations that exercised---extended beyond 21 years exerted of grief and evident statements of dispirited activity that occurred, unreasonably, during my youth. Every clarified content has been documented for the reader to decide his or her opinion to withdraw doubt and judgment, to accept my exhibiting character courageous for the brave fight, I had to contest through often silent and other times difficult challenges unspoken. I hesitated to testify fear of what was done to me. In conclusion of my book ***Crime, Control, and Captivity***, I never renounced my loyalty to consider sustaining my characterized faith, my authenticity of worship, and ability to profess excellent wisdom. Here is a parable that I recited and practiced, that I know, God has won the war for me against my enemies big and small, strong and egregious, against vulnerable defenses. Psalms 17:3 parable states : ***"You have tried my heart; You have visited me in the night. You have tested me and found no evil. I have resolved not to sin with the transgression of my mouth."*** Jesus Christ already determined the immaterial and material that is in our hearts. He is spirit. The spirit tests the hearts of men. He weighs the truth of our spirits how much is good and how much is evil. God discerns the irony what is pure and what is impure, but stays impartial. He's always present and balanced. He visits us in the night because of what the bible self-addresses; he is like a light that leads our path and validates closure. He lights our blindness to the mistakes we cannot detect, distinguishing what we can't see transparent in the night. He is the Alpha and Omega judge of the universe and by abiding bound authority, Lord, of universal law. He is spirit and truth if we convict ourselves confined to the conventionalism of Christ's law, putting aside the consequences of man's law not to sin the impurities from our mouths from His pure heart; vindicated in our actions, he still loves that person through obstruction being under attack. We're always being reconciled sincerity the inner-man made renewed inside outward the complete warrior of God. You can also backup the discipline system of natural sciences and say we renew our spirit by carbon dioxide breathed in the nose and released out of the mouth, manifests into oxygen converted is the spirit, by scientific analogy anecdote. By a convention of verified testimonial, God's covenant has an aspect shield of a sealed scientific philosophy of capital sovereignty. In fact Christ essentially integrates a symbolized jurisprudence of metaphysical liberty. The argument you can conclude, summarizes, he adapts a practicable---prosperity permanent. Here is another rule of thumb. If you buy something that is under warranty, you want to warrant experience of enjoyment every aspect you bought of that product in loyalty. Having significant wisdom, how do I apply that application? Well, for starters what impacts me I breakdown my tough fickle intelligently to avoid discombobulation of someone that forces me confusion. Sometimes you need to fight back constructive so you don't fall insecure, grasping strength that you can warrant protection against enemies. Fight back intelligently legal, not carelessly blunt. Final thought pondered. If you aspire to engineer work labor towards a group of goals for obtained entity of Constitutional entitlement, that is your profit. No ill-legitimate unlawful individual has the immoral obligation to deprive you of that earned benefit, the prize confiscated. *Never.* The declaration of Lord Jesus Christ is that one endless jurisdiction constituted above the universe.

Cory Morrel is an intermediary
author from Greenville, SC.
This is Cory's 3rd book publication from
his autobiography spotlight,
indicating inclusion authentic accounts
of instant experiences transpired.

<u>Previous Independent Best Seller Works</u>
<u>by Cory Morrel/Cory Morr:</u>

The Blue Sphere 2012 (Science-Fiction
Fantasy, Action, Adventure Novel).

SplashBreeze AngelPoint Path Destiny Collection-500
Psalm and Philosophies Affirmed Goal and Skills
Management Tool Book 2016 (NonFiction Psychology).

Crime, Control & Captivity 2021
(NonFiction Autobiography Memoir).

Printed in the United States
by Baker & Taylor Publisher Services